HC

MENSWEAR ILLUSTRATION

richard kilroy

MENSWEAR ILLUSTRATION

With 290 illustrations

 Thames & Hudson

On the jacket, front
Richard Haines
Prada A/W 2012–13
Created for *Il Palazzo*, 2014

On the jacket, back
Illustrations by Marco Klefisch (see
p. 187), Carlos Aponte (p. 28), Donald
Urquhart (p. 266), Tara Dougans
(p. 79), Martine Johanna (p. 169),
Howard Tangye (p. 246), Lee Song
(p. 195) and Richard Kilroy (p. 184).

Frontispiece
Julie Verhoeven
All Man
Created for *Ponystep* (UK), 2008

Profile of Richard Kilroy, p. 178, by Stuart Brumfitt, digital
news editor for *i-D* magazine and freelance journalist for
publications including *W, Dazed & Confused* and *The Guardian*.

First published in the United Kingdom in 2015 by
Thames & Hudson Ltd, 181A High Holborn,
London WC1V 7QX

Menswear Illustration © 2015 Thames & Hudson Ltd, London
Text © 2015 Richard Kilroy
Images © the illustrators

Designed by Karolina Prymaka

British Library Cataloguing-in-Publication Data
A catalogue record for this book is available from
the British Library

ISBN 978-0-500-51779-6

Printed and bound in China by Toppan Leefung Printing
Limited

To find out about all our publications, please visit
www.thamesandhudson.com. There you can subscribe
to our e-newsletter, browse or download our current catalogue,
and buy any titles that are in print.

contents

foreword

Dan Thawley

Editor-in-chief, *A Magazine Curated By*

Today the runway is a circus, and a canvas for many hundreds of amateur images whose questionable value is diffused for instant gratification across social media networks the world over. In fashion, close to all patience has been forgotten; however amidst the flashing, and clicking, and posting, sit a quiet few – their eyes flickering between paper and cloth, catching the intimate nuances and fleeting facets of a collection that are so often lost in the hyper-speed world of the internet.

Through the fug of excess in today's visual landscape, illustration shines as a clear beacon of pure and unadulterated creative expression. Concerned with line and shade, drawing distils a fashion moment as a fleeting artist's impression – where details fall aside to allow sweeping gestures of silhouette and bold colour to capture the bare bones of a designer's creation. Negative space is vital, framing the scene with a unique and subjective eye, be it a filter for the crowded atmospheres of a runway setting or a reflection of the calm, constructed set that an illustration sitting allows.

Hovering behind this incongruently tranquil medium is the menswear illustrator, whose scope it seems is narrowed even further. Menswear, as a rule, lacks the extravagance of its better half. The luxury is discreet, introverted. A patterned suit, a swinging coat, perhaps colourful sportswear or the opulence of a dandy – these are the few liberties that the artist may work with. The pages hereafter are testament to the gifts of these characters dedicated to exploding the boundaries of this vibrant art, their aesthetics as strangely beautiful and disparate as the designers' work they choose to draw. From established industry names to obscure global newcomers, *Menswear Illustration* captures our renewed fascination with fashion drawing, through the eyes of a new generation whose talent transmutes their sartorial musings into contemporary works of art.

Matthew Bell wears Matthew Miller S/S 2013
Richard Kilroy for *Decoy* (UK), 2013

introduction

Menswear is having a moment

Since the beginning of the twenty-first century there has been a huge rise in global interest in menswear, accompanied by an explosion in male grooming and sartorial blogging and an increase in men's fashion publications. In turn these have resulted in a greater focus on the illustration of menswear. Sales of menswear are set to overtake those of womenswear in the United Kingdom by 2016, and market research shows that British men already spend more on footwear than women do. Worldwide, the menswear market is expected to have increased by nearly 15 per cent over the period 2009–2014.

Back in 2004 Tom Ford had not yet set up a menswear label, nor had Fashion East's Lulu Kennedy started the highly influential collective show MAN with Gordon Richardson of Topman; Hedi Slimane was yet to publish *London Birth of a Cult*, with his photographs of Pete Doherty, and the much-imitated magazine *Fantastic Man* was still to launch. Since then men's identities and dress codes have not just evolved but also given birth to new styles, both on the catwalk and on the street. The cultural commentator Charlie Porter, who moved from *The Guardian* to *GQ* magazine in 2004, reflected on his website in 2014 on the advance of the menswear industry: 'Ten years since I started focusing solely on menswear. What's changed? Everything.'

On the catwalk, designers including Riccardo Tisci (for Givenchy), Jeremy Scott and Raf Simons (for Adidas) and Christopher Shannon have been influential in the rise of streetwear in high fashion. Then there is the cult of Rick Owens and his dark underworld; and Miuccia Prada and Yohji Yamamoto continue their multigenerational casting (Prada's show for Autumn/Winter 2012–13 even featured A-list film stars including Gary Oldman, Willem Dafoe and Adrien Brody). There are heavily tattooed and pierced 'alternative' street models, such as Jimmy Q and Josh Beech, the latter of whom was photographed by Slimane in 2008 for a *Vogue Hommes International* cover that was one of the most celebrated of the decade.

Advertisement
Tom Purvis for Austin Reed (UK), *c*. 1935

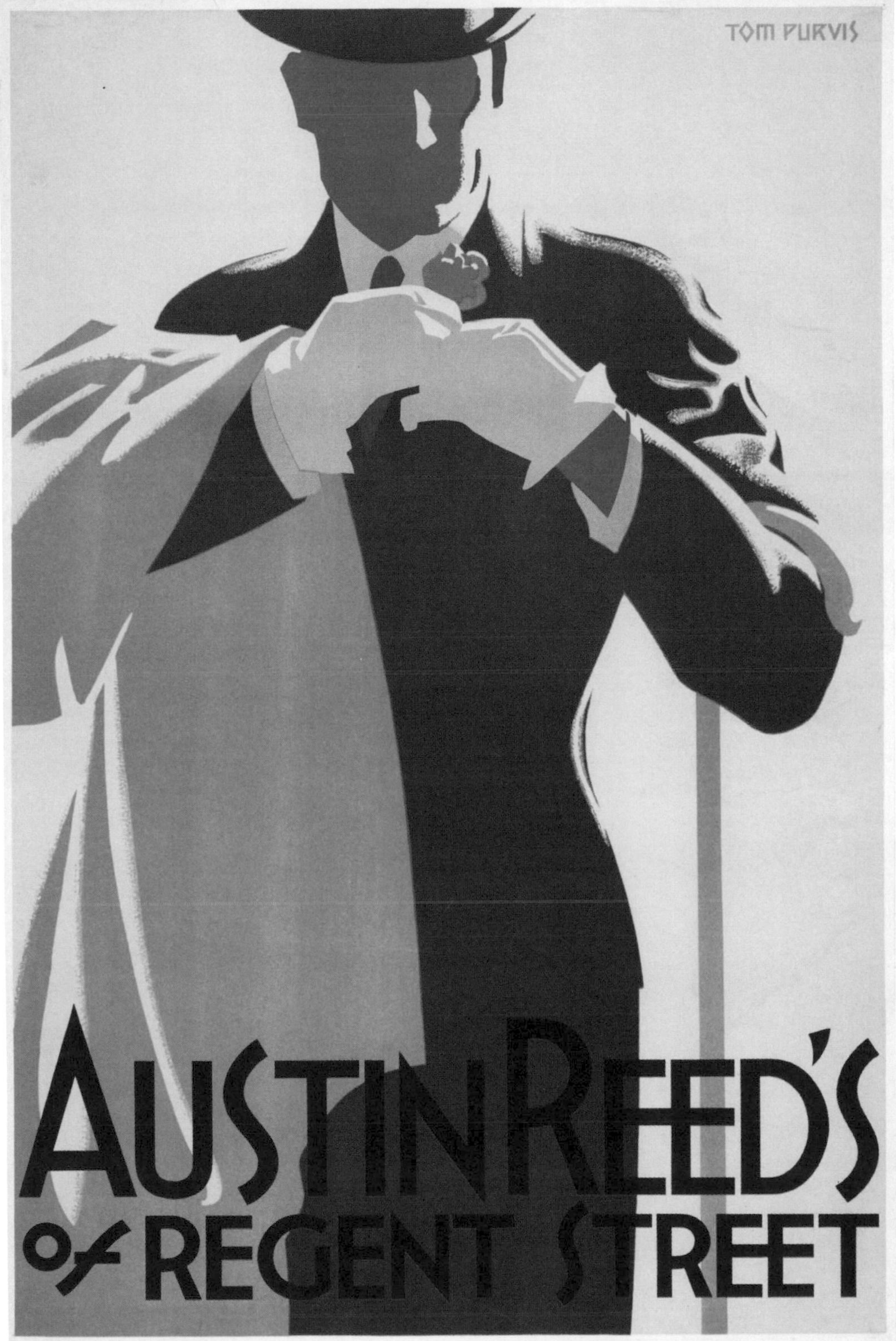
TOM PURVIS
AUSTIN REED'S
of REGENT STREET

Burberry catalogue, 1914

The buff male models of the 1990s were steadily replaced by younger, skinny, androgynous men, referred to as 'svelte princelings' by *Vogue*'s Hamish Bowles. Often credited to Slimane's influential street casting for Yves Saint Laurent and Dior Homme, and to the aesthetic of Raf Simons, the look would become the ideal of the male industry throughout the 2000s. By the 2010s, it had fleshed out to become more athletic, if still slim and young.

In recent times, we have seen the men of the Pitti Uomo fashion fair dressed in their dandy tailoring, snapped outside the shows by such bloggers as Tommy Ton of 'Jak & Jil'; the boys of east London with their myriad of continuously evolving looks; and the newly coined term 'hipster', referring to the Western subculture of men influenced by numerous other subcultures, such as grunge, beat, emo and hippy.

The history of menswear illustration

Men's fashion has always been far more regimented than women's, encumbered with strict codes of social etiquette and status. From the beginning of the twentieth century until the 1960s, such artists as J.C. Leyendecker, Tom Purvis, Jean Dulac and Marjac were among the leaders in illustrating the contemporary fashionable man. Their detailed works depicted well-dressed, aspirational gentlemen enjoying the downtime of their luxury living. Before the 1960s, the predominant subject matter of menswear fashion illustrations tended to be the aristocracy and members of the upper echelons of society. Successful fashion illustration was aesthetically bound up in portraying minute detail, rather than an expressive artistic outlet. In the 1920s and 1930s – often referred to as the 'golden age' of fashion illustration – Condé Nast required the artists who contributed to *Vogue* to report faithfully on the spirit of contemporary fashion, and complained that illustrators 'were chiefly interested in achieving amusing drawings and decorative effects,

Men's fashion illustration
Unknown artist, early 20th century

POUR CHEZ SOI

A chaque heure de la journée correspond un costume approprié. Les robes de chambre qui, durant un temps, ont subi une éclipse, ont retrouvé leur vogue. En voici d'originales :: :: :: :: :: en "cloky", légères, chaudes, et agréables à voir. :: :: :: ::

TISSUS DE MM. RODIER.

bored to death by faithful representation'. The arrival of photography may have relegated illustration to second place, but in doing so it freed illustrators from the constraints of reportage and allowed them to explore new, dynamic ways of interpreting the world of fashion.

Because of its history of rigid conformity, menswear did not experience as much attention as womenswear in the work of such famed illustrators as Erté, Andy Warhol and René Bouché. It is very difficult to find many images of men among their work and that of their contemporaries, although there are of course exceptions. Réjane Bargiel and Sylvie Nissen's book *Gruau: Portraits Of Men* (2012) revealed to the world the extent of René Gruau's contribution to drawing menswear, which far exceeded his infamous Dior Eau Sauvage advertisements and *Sir* magazine covers, and the depiction of men as simply props for his women. Gruau's man was far more sexy and relaxed, and at times humorous, than the 'modern' men produced by illustrators before him.

Similarly, the 'Peacock Revolution' of 1960s London – the youth culture movement named for its bright colours, bold flares, psychedelic suits and designs by the likes of Ossie Clark and Zandra Rhodes – had a huge impact on the work and wardrobe of Antonio Lopez, who until then had focused on womenswear. From then on, Lopez relentlessly studied his male models and muses, creating influential editorials for such publications as *Gentleman's Quarterly* and *L'Uomo Vogue*, and treating both sexes with equal interest.

Nobody defined 1980s high fashion quite as precisely Tony Viramontes. His cover for Janet Jackson's album *Control* (1986) and his cover art for *The Face* during the Buffalo period of Ray Petri are perfect examples of his arresting and energetic images. His illustrations of male models were mostly personal work, in a style said to be influenced by drawing classes at Parsons School of Art and the School of Visual Arts in New York held by Steven Meisel, who encouraged extreme viewpoints and exaggerated poses, even modelling in the classes himself.

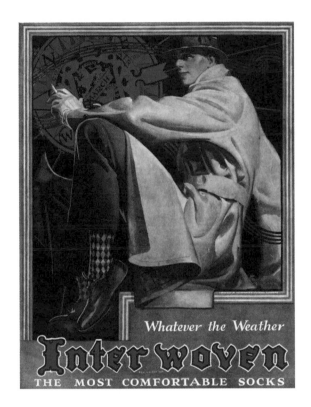

Advertisement
J.C. Leyendecker for Interwoven Socks
Hosiery (USA), 1920s

Opposite
Pour chez soi, illustration of men's
dressing gowns by Rodier
Marjac for *Monsieur* (France), 1921

We have a
beautiful seas-cape

Simpson
PICCADILLY

Swimwear advertisement
Unknown artist for Simpson of Piccadilly
(UK), 1960s

While Lopez and Viramontes both left the United States in order to immerse themselves in the renowned haute couture and fashion houses of Paris, the men and women depicted by the American poster artist Patrick Nagel became the defining image of commercial American fashion in the 1980s. Meanwhile, George Stavrinos's work for the *New York Times*, Bergdorf Goodman, the *Gentleman's Quarterly* and *Playboy*, with its extremely accomplished draughtsmanship and emphasis on chiaroscuro, harked back to Hollywood film noir of the 1940s and 1950s.

A highlight of the early 1980s, and a substantial platform for high-fashion illustration, was Anna Piaggi's *Vanity* magazine. Published in Italy by Condé Nast, and lasting for only ten issues because of its advertisers' concerns that it was too specialist, *Vanity* has attained the status of a cult collector's item. Within its pages, Piaggi regularly championed illustrators such as Lopez, and she was herself often drawn by Karl Lagerfeld, for whom she was something of a muse.

In the 1990s Thierry Perez's take on the energy and faces of the supermodel era saw him establish working relationships with both Jean Paul Gaultier and Azzedine Alaïa. His illustrations of Gianni Versace's male models with their big lips and even bigger chests are a perfect representation of the hyper-virile, muscular male supermodel of the time.

Fast-forwarding to contemporary fashion illustration, the *Vogue* cover illustrator David Downton has produced show invitations for Daks menswear, and live studies of such notable designers as Alber Elbaz and Stephen Jones relaxing at Claridge's Fumoir bar. These images resulted in the series 'Midnight at Noon (and Other Studies)' being exhibited at the London hotel. The drawings of Mathias Augustyniak of the design duo M/M (Paris) have served as covers and editorials for *Arena Homme+* and *Man About Town*, while Richard Haines's sketchily illustrated men are displayed in the windows of Bernie's in New York, in various leading men's publications and even on the catwalk itself (as part of Siki Im's menswear show for Spring/Summer 2014).

Portrait of Jesse Harris
Tony Viramontes for Gotamex (France), 1984

In recent years the relevance of fashion illustration has been acknowledged with an array of exhibitions, both contemporary and retrospective. In 2010 the exhibition 'Drawing Fashion' ran at the Design Museum in London, and late that same year Somerset House, also in London, displayed the show 'Dior Illustrated: René Gruau and the Line of Beauty'. New books dedicated to such artists as Lopez and Viramontes were accompanied by exhibitions in New York and Milan.

In 2007 the Fashion Illustration Gallery was founded in London to promote and sell original artworks and prints by artists in the field. In 2013, in a testament to the growing commercial interest in fashion illustration among collectors, it collaborated with Christie's auction house and Issa London on a unique exhibition of original works by David Downton, Tanya Ling, Richard Haines, Mats Gustafson, Richard Gray, Gary Card, Jean-Philippe Delhomme and Ricardo Fumanal, among others. Such exhibitions are a sign of the wider acceptance of fashion illustration as a distinguished art form in its own right, and, as if to give the final seal of approval to the genre, since 2011 the Victoria and Albert Museum in London has actively sought to acquire original works by contemporary illustrators for its archives.

The differences between illustrating menswear and womenswear

The illustration of menswear is nothing new, and yet very few publications have so far focused on it, perhaps because menswear in its conformity has lived in the shadow of womenswear. However, the recent changes in attitude mean that a new spectrum of inspired artists are now keen to interpret the work of the new generation of designers. When I was interviewed by the editor of *Port* magazine, David Hellqvist, in 2013 about an issue of my publication, *Decoy*, that focused on menswear illustration, Hellqvist pointed out that it was almost as though 'the beautiful threads of [the] mentioned designers take on a Sideshow Bob role...

Trousers by Gianni Versace
Tony Viramontes, 1984

merely a means to the end. The purpose is as much to showcase drawing as it is to drool over Meadham Kirchhoff's SS13 collection.'

It could be asked why this book should focus on menswear, when it might be more rational to reflect illustration as a whole. This is not, after all, a 'how-to' book on drawing the male figure. But when we examine those artists who concentrate on menswear, we find particular emphases, moods and styles that are idiosyncratic to the craft. The sinuous lines and fluidity of materials that are commonly used to convey the draping and curves of womenswear are not necessarily suited to menswear. Different visual symbolism is at play, and muscles, shoulders and hands, strength and a different type of posture are often to the fore. That is not to say, however, that all the men depicted by these artists are traditionally masculine. Indeed, as in fashion and – to a greater extent – in real life, they range from the muscular and powerful, through the well-groomed sartorial gent, to the more effeminate, younger, slim guy, and can be fully dressed or fully undressed, or anything in between.

Menswear illustration today

The street-cast men of Richard Gray are often heavily tattooed, their hunched shoulders and undeniable erotic charge dominating the frame. Peter Turner's slender boys, meanwhile, with their model attributes, stretch out and recline in their underwear, striking a balance between a contemporary underwear editorial and figurative art. The uniquely narrative style of Graham Samuels's work for *Fashion Tale* magazine is unusual among photographic editorial, let alone illustration, in its structure, which is more akin to that of a graphic novel. Different again are Tara Dougans's imperfect men, with their long hair, monobrows, pimples, glares and strong, angular proportions – the antithesis of the preened boys one would expect in a glossy editorial.

Angelo Colon
Antonio Lopez, 1983

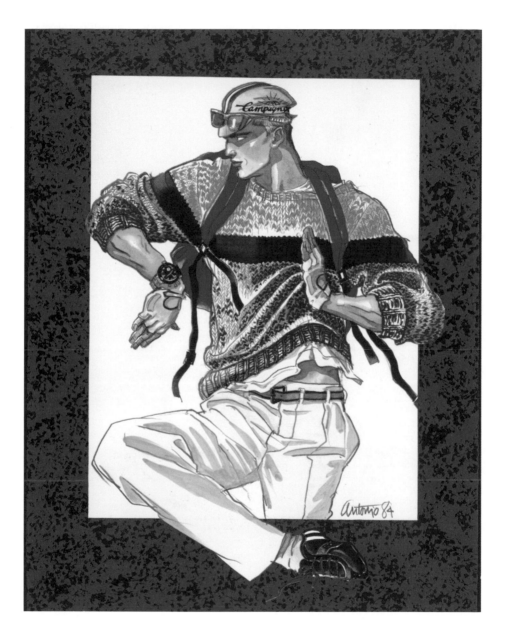

Antonio Lopez for *Gentleman's Quarterly*
(USA), 1984

It should be remembered that the phrase 'fashion illustration' does not necessarily signify the portrayal of a dressed figure; it is more suitable and creatively open to say that it refers to illustration *in the context of* fashion. This is true of both menswear and womenswear, and the field as a whole. The artist Donald Urquhart, known for his black-and-white pen-and-ink

Advertisement
George Stavrinos for Devereaux, 1982

Opposite
Baroque Boy
Thierry Perez for Gianni Versace, 1991

drawings of tarnished glamour, drag queens and ageing Hollywood starlets, offers a particularly refreshing take with his work for *Ponystep* magazine, featured in this book. Urquhart frequently depicts neither colour nor fit, yet his works nevertheless provide a brilliantly original interpretation. The abstract shapes of Helen Bullock and Julie Verhoeven have the same effect, offering new notions of what it is to create a 'fashion illustration', whether it be inspired by a male model, a particular attribute or the abstract interpretation of a stylized man.

PERRY ELLIS

Award-winning women's-wear designer Ellis has only recently broadened his scope to menswear. His approach is decidedly un-traditional. "I do not believe in fashion trends. I believe only in personal style and freedom of choice. For spring '81, I am working on loose, easy separates and hope to provide a man with new, interesting and amusing alternatives to choose from."

The most lucid area in which fashion illustration has resurfaced is reportage. We are now living in an age of globalization and a world of immediacy, and we have come to expect information within seconds. We no longer wait for the seasonal reports to come out in magazines; instead they are live-streamed and interactive, and so there are many sources of information. The huge surge in online show reports and the greater immediacy of information have led many publications to seek more diverse and broad-ranging material for their online counterparts. Before this explosion of documenting shows and the related field of street style, illustration as reportage was sometimes referred to longingly, as a distant memory blotted out by the advent of photography. However, a sweet irony is that most publications now strive for original coverage, commissioning such artists as Matthew Attard Navarro, Richard Haines and Clym Evernden, who are undeniably at the forefront of this current wave. Jean-Philippe Delhomme, meanwhile, was arguably at the head of the movement more than twenty years ago; his continuously influential work and, more recently, his blog 'The Unknown Hipster' have meant that he retains a position of influence to this day.

The artists featured in this book are renowned internationally for work that ranges from street-style reportage, designer's sketches and editorial illustration to commissioned portraits and the figurative study of models and muses. It is by turns imaginative, decorative, aggressive and surreal.

Designers as illustrators

Unlike other publications on fashion illustrators, this book features the work of current menswear designers as well as that of contemporary illustrators. As a fashion illustrator, I am equally inspired by the sketches of designers, whether it be from their graduate portfolios, part of their design line-ups or just an offhand sketch, and it is stimulating to see how much such pieces vary

Perry Ellis look by Patrick Nagel,
Playboy **(USA), 1981**

and how impressive they are as works in their own right. They provide a unique glimpse of personal work that is often unseen. Many fashion illustrators famed for their commercial work have a background in fashion design that has informed their style. Laird Borrelli's book *Fashion Illustration by Fashion Designers* (2008) showcases some great examples of designers' creative drawing, and it is to be hoped that interest will continue to grow in this area.

It is worth noting the difference between a designer's creative drawing and the type of technical drawing needed to produce a garment. For designers, making creative illustrations is an introverted and intimate process, which immerses them in a character and a world that embodies the look they are aiming for; it is admittedly a luxury for many established designers. Aitor Throup's widely praised design process almost always starts with his unique illustrations of twisted figures, which become the inspiration for his collections.

The emerging designer Fiongal Greenlaw, a graduate of the Royal College of Art, London, explains that when he was at the RCA, 'my illustrations became so synonymous with my designs that one would often push the other, and this is where I had the time and opportunity to really explore and develop my techniques. The most immediate and supportive comments would often come in regards to my drawings.' As a result of his distinctive images, he is in the unusual position of having illustrations commissioned separately from his design portfolio.

Howard Tangye, formerly head of womenswear at Central Saint Martins College of Art and Design, London, works as a life-drawing artist and interestingly notes that clothes are not his primary focus when developing his practice. He emphasizes the importance of understanding the figure from the inside out, which allows an individual style to develop. It is his firm belief that one cannot teach a drawing 'style', but rather that an artist grows into one.

This book explores not only the leaders of fashion illustration and the private sketches of menswear designers, but also their perceptions as visual artists of the modern man and of modern fashions, and how these contribute to menswear. There is as much reason to celebrate men in fashion illustration as there has ever been in photography and fine art.

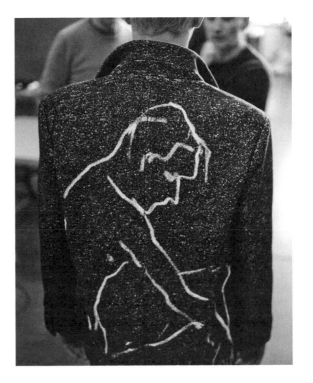

carlos aponte

What I like about drawing men or menswear is that I can be aggressive, bold and full of character. Women are the great illusionists. Men are more revealing, raw; I find everything in men more pronounced and unapologetic.

One of the few illustrators today able to work in a multitude of styles, Puerto Rican artist Carlos Aponte creates works – often (but not always) monochromatic – that share a graphic quality and simplicity. Aponte, whose work is characterized by strong lines and a strong sense of composition, sees the influence of Expressionism as a constant in his work. His understanding of how to interpret fabric and cut is crucial to an approach that would not succeed at the hands of a less well-trained artist.

Aponte studied at Parsons The New School for Design and the Fashion Institute of Technology in New York, and now lectures at the latter. Of his two great mentors, Antonio Lopez and Jack Potter, he says: '[They were] two different fashion illustrators with different points of view. Antonio taught me about line and fluidity, and Jack [taught me] about shape and character.' The work of the early twentieth-century American photographer George Platt Lynes is also a key influence.

Aponte works fast, an approach that he believes is important in keeping things fresh. In what he describes as a 'sculptural' process, he makes the pieces in his masking-tape series by ripping, cutting and manipulating the tape to create texture and shadow. He also works in ink and digitally. He explains his philosophy: 'I must always try to be honest and faithful to the line. To me lines and shapes are everything. I...tell my students that's the key to being a good illustrator...I don't have a specific creative influence because it's everywhere. It could be a shadow of a person standing on a corner or a new piece of music, a mood, but most of all a feeling.'

DJ portraits
Created for *FLAUNT* (USA), 2013

Opposite
Untitled
Personal work, 2012

carlos aponte

This page and opposite
Untitled
Created for Gilbert and Lewis, 2012

artaksiniya

I love drawing menswear because it has become more provocative recently; it now has that touch of healthy weirdness. Drawing men is always an adventure for me. I don't know how it feels to be a man, so it becomes way more interesting because of the complexity.

The eclectic style of the Moscow-based illustrator Artaksiniya fuses clear lines, bold colours and excessive graphic elements. She professes a love of Modernism, but reverts to decadent imagery in her work. The artists Aubrey Beardsley and Gustav Klimt had a huge impact on her as a child, and she is also a great admirer of traditional Chinese art. This is borne out in her ornate images, many of which depict otherworldly men and women, sometimes with elongated necks, green skin and exaggerated proportions, and which are also reminiscent of the work of illustrators Mel Odom and Richard Gray.

Interestingly, Artaksiniya's background is journalistic – she studied journalism and literature for six years – and she began her career in illustration in a small way for newspaper articles. At the same time she produced dynamic personal work involving men, women and all things fashion, with a distinctive approach to pattern and ornament. Despite being a relative newcomer to the industry, she now boasts an intimidatingly consistent portfolio of beautiful characters and graphic prints, all fleshed out in ballpoint pen, pencil and paint.

According to Artaksiniya, whose approach has always been one of curiosity, a fashion collection must have 'something irregular' about it in order to draw her attention: 'Be it shape or colour-block, I need something to engage my imagination. I have a soft spot for accessories, especially in menswear, since they're becoming more and more peculiar and radical each season. Once I see anything extraordinary – strange-looking hats, metal teeth, masks – I fall in love and immediately start weaving my picture around it. As an artist, I love clothes to be strange, and I'm always grateful for collections that contain elegance, humour and an invitation to exaggerate the idea for the sake of a striking picture.'

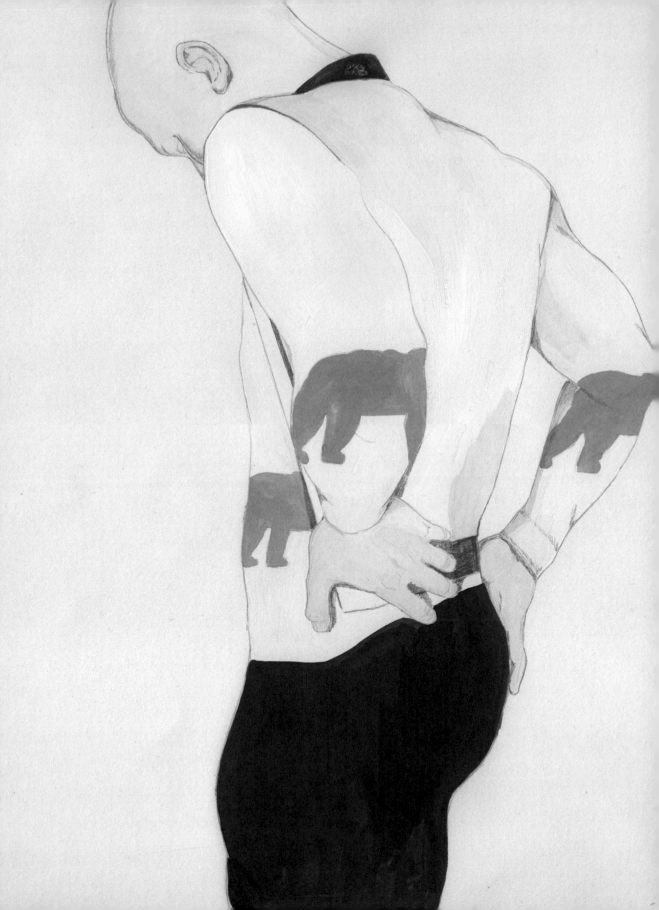

Above
Bobby Abley A/W 2014–15
Created for SHOWstudio.com, 2014

Right
Astrid Andersen A/W 2014–15
Created for SHOWstudio.com, 2014

Opposite
Christopher Raeburn A/W 2014–15
Created for SHOWstudio.com, 2014

Comme des Garçons S/S 2013
Personal work, 2012

Opposite
Alexander McQueen A/W 2011–12
Personal work, 2011

This page and opposite
Meadham Kirchhoff S/S 2013
Created for *Decoy* (UK), 2013

matthew attard navarro

Illustration comes naturally to me and I like to work fast; I know the only way I can hold my focus is if I illustrate someone instantaneously. I definitely prefer street-style illustration to sittings. I believe fashion is on the streets.

One of many illustrators whose rapid-fire sketches have caught the zeitgeist for online reportage, Maltese artist Matthew Attard Navarro has been commissioned to produce his Moleskine diary layouts for *Dazed & Confused*'s 'Dazed Digital' show reports. At art college in Malta he was always pushed to explore a quick style of working and to deliver a large body of work, and that training is evident in his drawing style, which shows a fast hand and sharp observation.

Attard Navarro has previously run a Malta-based design studio. Since moving to London and joining VICE Media as art director, he has worked with various fashion and luxury brands on innovative campaigns. Based in London, he now works with the Net-A-Porter Group and is creative director of *Platinum Love* magazine, a digital cultural publication that he founded in 2007 while at the University of Malta. In 2012 he launched the Platinum Institute, Malta's own centre for fashion education, and, although it is still in its research phase, by 2018 he aims to give many the opportunity to go beyond the academic side of fashion and straight into the industry.

Attard Navarro has built up a varied portfolio of art direction, design, illustration and photography, but he has always preferred illustration using pen and paper: 'I work through my Moleskines as if I'm reading a comic. I tend to fill one or two books during fashion weeks and I tend to keep my imagery in a landscape format, as if it were a street-style image. Photography requires much more work, a model, film and a camera. Illustration...is my long-time outlet for creativity. I was illustrating at school from the age of eight, and still am today. I can do it very simply anywhere; all I need is a pen.'

Adrien Sahores wears Kenzo
Personal work, 2013

Opposite, top
Jean-Paul Paula wears Juun J
Personal work, 2013

Opposite, bottom
Miles McMillan and Paul Boche
Personal work, 2013

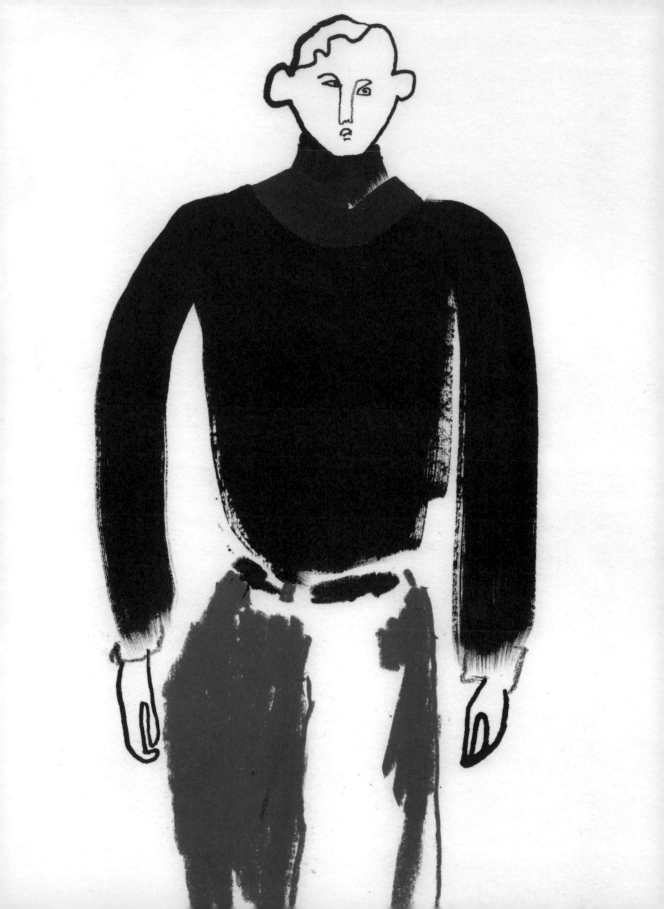

helen bullock

**I don't care much for convention in my drawings.
I work more from feeling and intuition. I try to live by
those rules, too...striving to be truthful and authentic,
embracing oddness and strength.**

Newcomer Helen Bullock has captivated audiences with her work for the likes of SHOWstudio and *1883* magazine. Her spontaneous style has made her the perfect candidate for reportage, and she is part of a new wave of illustrators being commissioned by the online counterpart sites of prolific magazines, including *AnOther* and *A Magazine Curated By*. She is admired for her loosely interpreted, rather than purely descriptive illustrations, sometimes drawn at the shows themselves; her style is intuitive, spontaneous and naïve, and now more frequently painterly. It flouts the tradition of calculated figurative studies, and instead highlights certain attributes of an outfit in order to explore it in colour and line.

For the refreshingly honest Bullock, who studied womenswear at Central Saint Martins College of Art and Design in London and is now a visiting lecturer there, the appeal of mens-wear lies in 'clean lines, colour palettes and the hot chiselled models'. More often than not her male figures possess strong shoulders, offset with faces that appear awkward and odd.

Bullock's peers attest that her character and presence are just as colourful as her work. 'I feel at a low if I'm not wearing brightness,' she said in an interview for the blog 'Design & Culture by Ed' in November 2013. 'As I was working on the drawings after the shows, I did wonder "Is there any point to this?", seeing as there are a trillion photos of this one look on the internet. It just felt like an indulgence. However, maybe that's the point: perhaps the one illustration as a personal response can be equally powerful. It's a more tangible piece, more of an artwork than a function.' Bullock's exuberant sense of colour lends itself to the production of bold print-led clothing and other textiles, which she produces under her own label and in collaboration, most recently with the American brand Anthropologie.

Above
Shaun Samson S/S 2014
Created for *Used Magazine* (UK), 2014

Right
J.W. Anderson S/S 2014
Created for *Used Magazine* (UK), 2014

Opposite
J.W. Anderson A/W 2013–14
Created for SHOWstudio.com, 2013

helen bullock

helen bullock

helen bullock
48

Above
Alexander McQueen S/S 2014
Created for *Used Magazine*, 2014

Right
Lee Roach S/S 2014
Created for *Used Magazine*, 2014

Opposite
Jil Sander A/W 2013–14
Created for SHOWstudio.com, 2013

From 'Inflate Redux'
Created for *Dazed & Confused*
(UK), 2010

gary card

**My illustrations jump between two conflicting styles,
one a very raw, impulsive, almost jagged painterly style,
the other a twisted take on the cartoon iconography
of my youth. My fashion illustration style tends
to focus on process and immediacy.**

Gary Card's inky figures display the interest in three-dimensional form that appears in his sculptures of faces and abandoned amusement parks and which has earned him a reputation as one of fashion's most in-demand set designers. His work encompasses campaigns, installations and editorials for Stella McCartney, Cos, *Vogue Hommes Japan*, *Dazed & Confused*, *i-D* and Dover Street Market, among others, as well as illustrations for Liberty of London, *Visionaire* and *AnOther* magazine, and headwear for Lady Gaga and for the Comme des Garçons Spring/Summer 2012 collection.

London-based Card – a self-confessed nerd – is obsessed with comics and sci-fi. A child of the 1990s, he spent 'hours hopping between MTV, Nickelodeon and any sci-fi B-movie rubbish that was on, and that is still all over the stuff I create'. He studied theatre design at Central Saint Martins College of Art and Design, and his influences range from Jean Paul Gaultier to *Star Trek*, from Paul McCarthy and Louise Bourgeois to Jim Woodring and James Jean. Totem poles, distressed, elongated figures, surreal cartoon characters and mechanical animals all feature in his work, which experiments playfully with colour, and he has what he describes as 'a bizarre compulsion for drawing hysterical-looking clowns, all sweaty and panicked'. As a set designer, Card draws quickly, thinking less about style than about describing the design in the clearest way possible. He suggests that this is why his fashion illustration is so aggressive and textural, as he allows himself to be more expressive and impulsive.

Card's illustrations for *Dazed & Confused* shown here are from a photo shoot with the stylist Robbie Spencer. Card produced outfits inspired by William S. Burroughs's novel *Naked Lunch* (1959) and by the film director David Cronenberg, with unusual padded pieces, headgear and plaster accessories.

This page and opposite
From 'Inflate Redux'
Created for *Dazed & Confused*
(UK), 2010

Portrait of Paul Newman
Created for *I Like My Style Quarterly*
(Germany), 2010

guglielmo castelli

**My men originate from a space without time;
they are fluid forms and without age,
but they embody the essence of reality.**

In his work for *Vogue Italia* online, Turin-based illustrator Guglielmo Castelli uses materials more akin to those required for fine art, such as oil or acrylic paint on board. Indeed, he has produced a large number of works that have featured in galleries in Italy. His work embodies the very fine line that exists today between the defining qualities of an artist and those of an illustrator. We see illustrations in art galleries, and paintings in magazines; many illustrators can be classed as artists, and vice versa. In any case, 'art' and 'illustration' are equal. The fundamental difference lies in the fact that an artist creates for the sake of their own expression, while an illustrator, although expressing their own taste stylistically, creates for clients.

In an age when original pieces by the most successful fashion illustrators sell at high prices under auction to collectors, Castelli's work shares this crossover appeal, and it is easy to see why. His tortured, twisted figures and the play between two-dimensional and three-dimensional perspective are reminiscent of the work of Francis Bacon and the contemporary Japanese pop artist Yoshitomo Nara. Flat areas of bold colour and a general sense of isolation and melancholy are common traits in his illustrations. The characters hover between childhood and adulthood in a surreal and engaging way, their morphing shapes appearing lost and contemplative.

While some of the figures in Castelli's personal work seem to be suffering – their faces obscured or facing away from the viewer – the characters in his fashion illustrations are lighter in mood, less contorted and even occasionally smiling. Among a wide variety of designers, his simultaneously cerebral and playful portfolio consistently features the clothes of Prada and Comme des Garçons.

Child
Personal work, 2012

Opposite
Givenchy
Personal work, 2011

guglielmo castelli

guglielmo castelli

Right
Portrait of Alexander McQueen
Created for *I Like My Style Quarterly*
(Germany), 2010

Below
Portrait of Martin Margiela
Created for *I Like My Style Quarterly*
(Germany), 2010

Opposite
Prada A/W 2010–11
Created for private client, 2011

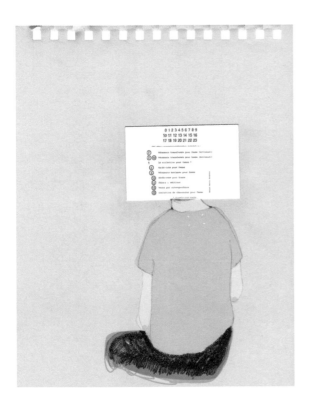

sam cotton

**My desire to produce something intriguing
to the viewer is constant, it's just that my method
and my route can be quite different between
the media of design and illustration.**

The designer Sam Cotton is no stranger to the world of illustration, having studied it at university. It was after that, while he was producing prints as an intern for Alexander McQueen in 2008, that he met Agi Mdumulla, who was working with the McQueen men's design team. In 2010 they joined forces to set up their own label, Agi & Sam, and were awarded the Emerging Talent menswear prize at the British Fashion Awards after just three solo shows and a collaboration with Topman. The label, one of the biggest success stories in British menswear in recent years, was also nominated for the International Woolmark Prize and in 2014 won Breakthrough Designer at the GQ Men of the Year awards.

Cotton's illustrations shown here were produced as an original and personal response to the Agi & Sam Spring/Summer 2015 collection, which was showcased using red- and auburn-haired models with freckles. His style is elegant in its sparing simplicity. A mixture of hand-drawn and digital, Cotton's playful compositions are an exercise in graphic form rather than a dedicated expression of the collection itself. Although Cotton does not think of himself as a working illustrator, his background in the field continues in his print work for the label: 'I've always liked to try and do as little as possible to the illustration and not work into it too much. I try to use small elements of the illustration to tell more about the subject, rather than filling all the negative space with unnecessary detail. Sometimes the space itself can be more intriguing than the entirety of the illustration. With print in particular I try to evoke something different from the textile, whereas with illustration I try to be quite subdued and minimal.'

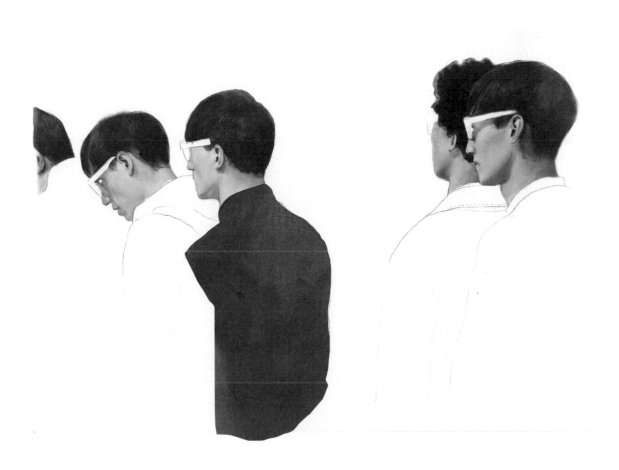

This page and opposite
Agi & Sam S/S 2015
Personal work, 2014

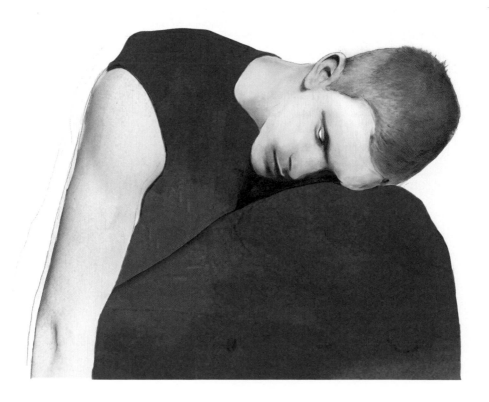

sam cotton

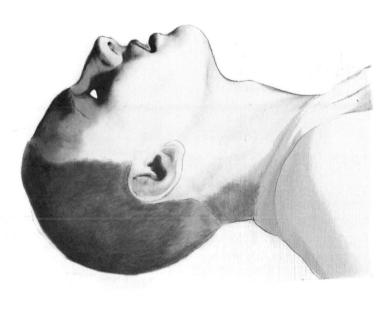

jean-philippe delhomme

I'm interested in representing the signs of the time in the small details of an attitude, not just the fashion...the way it's worn, and what it says about a character...Fashion is temporary, but human body language and behaviour are eternal.

Internationally acclaimed in various fields including art, writing, animation, blogging and illustrating, Jean-Philippe Delhomme is most aptly described as a social and cultural commentator. During his celebrated career, which began in the late 1980s when his work first appeared in *Vogue*, his vivid *mise en scènes* have done more than simply document the fashion industry's social scene. His figures may be from the upper echelons of the style world, but Delhomme's witty, humorous observations elegantly and good-naturedly satirize the industry's pretensions.

Delhomme's blog, 'The Unknown Hipster' (a satirical pseudonym), presents his observation of the comings and goings of fashion and urban crowds in a simpler, more direct pencil style than his commercial work. It led to a book of the same name, published in 2012. Delhomme's other publications include *Art Contemporain* (2001), *Le Drame de la Déco* (2000), *Design Addicts* (2007), *The Cultivated Life* (2009) and the children's book *Visit to Another Planet* (2000). A graduate in animation from the École Nationale Supérieure des Arts Décoratifs, Paris, he has also directed animated films for commercial clients.

New York is important to Delhomme. Although he currently lives in Paris, the 'Big Apple' is something of a second home, where his studio and many clients are and where he feels his greatest work is done. It is no surprise that he was asked to produce the illustrations for the New York edition of Louis Vuitton's travel books in 2013. His witty Parisian perspective has also won over *GQ USA*'s columnist Glenn O'Brien, who replaced photography with Delhomme's work for his column 'Style Guy'. (Delhomme also contributes regularly to *GQ*'s French edition.) Delhomme's other clients include the *LA Times*, the *New York Times*, *W Magazine*, *Interview* magazine, *Vogue*, *House & Garden*, Barneys New York and Sotheby's. His work has been exhibited in Paris, New York, Berlin, Munich, Hyères (France), London and Tokyo.

Man on a Motorbike/What Would Be the
Appropriate Bag to Ride a Motorbike?
Created for the Style Guy, *GQ* (USA), 2013

Man in Pink Suit
Created for *GQ* (France), 2013

Above
Man on the Catwalk
Created for El Palacio de Hierro, 2012

Right
Man on the Catwalk
Created for El Palacio de Hierro, 2012

Opposite
Louis Vuitton and Prada S/S 2014
Created for *Série Limitée (Les Echos)*, 2012

jean-philippe delhomme

stephen doherty

**I like that the men I draw often end up resembling caricatures
of people I know. I start by drawing one feature, then build
around it and see what happens. My subjects tend
to be fans of print and have strong noses and big ears.**

After studying at Central Saint Martins College of Art and Design in London, designer and artist Stephen Doherty began his career as first design assistant for the innovative knitwear label Craig Lawrence. Leaving after six seasons to concentrate on his own work and focus once more on drawing, he quickly began to exhibit in group shows in London, as well as at the independent galleries Secret Project Robot in New York and PERCY in San Francisco.

Doherty is noted for his emotionally charged figures and sensitive colour palettes, often broken up with manic mark-making. His illustrations, in pencil, crayon, watercolour and acrylic, are frequently hurried and expressive. The image is often distorted in favour of an intuitive approach to mark-making and colour, resulting in a dynamic, characteristic style. When he is not working to a brief, his drawings are lively and fluid but not greatly detailed: 'I prefer to give an impression [and] make people want to see the clothes for themselves.'

In Doherty's series 'Sauna Faces', he cast a set of characters as a mixture of regulars, one-offs and first-timers at an imaginary sauna. The series was picked up by SHOWstudio and exhibited alongside the work of such artists as Marina Abramovic, Franko B and the Gao Brothers. Now a regular contributor to SHOWstudio, he has also collaborated with international brands including Maison Martin Margiela, Mary Katrantzou, MAC Cosmetics and Beefeater gin, and with the stylists Katy Shillingford and Anna Trevelyan.

Doherty's debut fashion collection, *The Deadhouse* (Autumn/Winter 2014), encompassed many disciplines, including drawing, printmaking and set design, and was exhibited at Somerset House in London. In it, his layered, printed-leather garments were displayed both on models and alongside his illustrations, translating his free style and artisanal approach to materials into pattern and becoming wearable art.

Stephen Doherty A/W 2014–15
Personal work, 2014

Opposite, left
Craig Green A/W 2014–15
Personal work, 2014

Opposite, right
Stephen Doherty A/W 2014–15
Personal work, 2014

stephen doherty
74

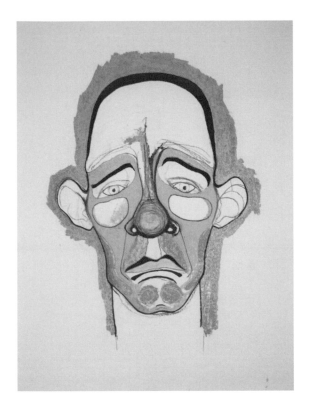

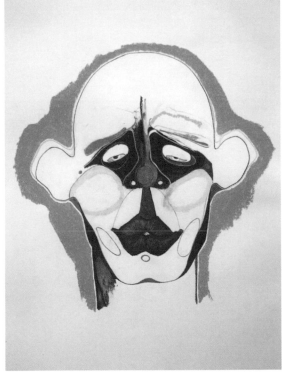

This page
Pop. Pill. Kiss.
Personal work, 2011

Opposite
No Takers for Peter
Personal work, 2011

tara dougans

**Menswear somehow feels more open to
interpretation – visually its delivery tends
to be more subtle than womenswear,
so a little twist goes a long way.**

The unique identity of Tara Dougans's male figures comes from their strikingly original profiles: they are androgynous, young and imperfect. Monobrows, post-pubescent moustaches and spots are not uncommon. Neither everyday men nor typical male models, they could be considered a reflection of the contemporary fascination with alternative casting. Beguiling stares and awkward expressions render them aloof and assured, otherworldly and unattainable.

Dougans has lived in Toronto, London, Amsterdam and Berlin, and her curiosity for change has led her constantly to try out new approaches. She declares that the two most important components of her work are surprise and delight, both of which can be seen in her dynamic GIFs, which pair careful detailing with a subtle animated twist. They represent a relatively new direction in contemporary fashion illustration of which Dougans is at the forefront. She is acknowledged for pioneering the illustrated 'animated editorial' in her collaborations with SHOWstudio and the global cultural platform Nowness. Her works for *commons&sense* and *Varoom!* magazines featured here are portrayed as stills, but were originally animated, as can be seen online. Dougans has worked with Maison Martin Margiela for SHOWstudio, Iris van Herpen, Karl Lagerfeld, *The Telegraph*, Amsterdam International Fashion Week, Selfridges and the fashion department of the Royal Academy of Fine Arts, Antwerp.

The great appeal of Dougans's work lies not solely in its characters, but also in her meticulous attention to detail and composition. She explains that she often treats her work as design, rather than conventional illustration. A common trait is an obsessive, almost masochistic level of intricacy that is demonstrated in complicated prints and undulating swirls of hair. Despite her self-professed love of the unexpected, then, her works are clearly not quickly conceived, yet their impact is undeniable.

Above, left
Dior Homme A/W 2010–11
Personal work, 2010

Above, right
Dries Van Noten A/W 2010–11
Personal work, 2010

Opposite
Raf Simons A/W 2010–11
Personal work, 2010

tara dougans

This page and opposite
Prada A/W 2012–13
Created for *commons&sense*
(Japan), 2012

Miu Miu S/S 2010
Personal work, 2010

Opposite
The Fantastic Man (Tom Ford jacket)
Personal work, 2010

tara dougans

eduard erlikh

**The fluid line of my drawings and focus on the
body movement and its dynamics, rather than on
the face, come from my love of ballet and dance
theatre. I look on fashion as a fluid art form.**

Russian-born illustrator Eduard Erlikh is renowned for creating editorials for international publications including *Vogue*, *Marie Claire France*, *Elle Germany*, *Madame Figaro* and *W Magazine*. In an interview for the *Huffington Post* in November 2012, Erlikh described what he sees as the turning point of his career, when American *Vogue* offered him a contract: 'That was an awesome project with crazy deadlines, where I had to create up to twenty-four full-page images per issue.' His commercial clients include Lanvin, Tiffany & Co., Ann Taylor, Bloomingdale's, Van Cleef & Arpels, the New York Royalton Hotel, Clinique and the drinks manufacturer Cinzano. He has also designed ballet costumes, and in the spring of 2011 the Vienna State Opera Museum organized an exhibition of his work in that genre, 'Eduard Erlikh and Don Quixote'.

The international gallery Lumas, which sells some of Erlikh's pieces, describes his appeal: 'He is a master of the moment, and that is why it is impossible to tear your eyes from his works: you fear you might miss something despite being in the midst of the action.' His dynamic figures stretch, bend, strut and recline with great strength and versatility. His women are demure, elegant and self-assured. The men in his personal studio work are powerfully portrayed: often nude, sometimes erect, contorted in sexually alluring stances, with strong brows and an emphasis on muscles. Tattoos, cigarettes and hoop earrings are regular accessories.

Despite the fact that vivid and varied colours play a strong role in his work, at his core Erlikh is a purist. His appreciation for and mastery of line echo that of such great fashion illustrators as René Bouché, René Gruau and Henri de Toulouse-Lautrec (Erlikh's favourite painter, and an inspiration during his time at art school in Russia), resulting in a timeless appeal.

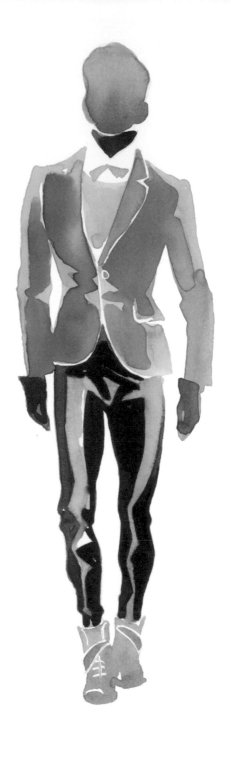

Junya Watanabe A/W 2011–12
Created for *Männer* (Germany), 2012

Opposite, left
Givenchy A/W 2011–12
Created for *Männer* (Germany), 2012

Opposite, right
Lanvin A/W 2011–12
Created for *Männer* (Germany), 2012

eduard erlikh

Gucci S/S 2010
Created for the Italian Trade
Commission, 2010

Opposite
Giorgio Armani S/S 2010
Created for the Italian Trade
Commission, 2010

Thom Browne A/W 2014–15
Created for *A Magazine Curated By*
(Belgium), 2014

clym evernden

**In terms of physical appearance I tend to go for guys
who have extreme proportions, whether it be a long fringe,
a big nose or gangly limbs. I am drawn to those who
have a natural or slightly inward/thoughtful quality
that I find interesting or can relate to.**

Clym Evernden is something of a fashion week darling. Journalists and editors cannot get enough of his live event illustration coverage, and his impressive list of clients includes *Vogue*, *Fantastic Man*, *AnOther* magazine, *Harper's Bazaar* and *The Telegraph*, Mulberry, Nicole Farhi, Zoë Jordan and Paul Smith. Evernden's background places him naturally in the field of fashion illustration. The son of illustrator Graham Evernden and artist Susan Evernden, he has a degree in English and fine art from the University of Exeter and studied womenswear at Central Saint Martins College of Art and Design in London. There he was taught illustration by Camilla Dixon and Howard Tangye, and won the Colin Barnes Illustration Award in 2003.

Evernden's continuing practice in ballet and former work as a model inform the physicality of his illustrations. The similarities between the worlds of fashion and ballet are obvious, not only in the concentrated form of models' and dancers' idealized and unattainable physiques, but also in the theatricality of both industries.

Evernden's fast, loose ink work has placed him at the forefront of illustrated show coverage, an area that is booming with the rise of online reporting. The immediacy of such pieces is part of the charm that has brought back a supposedly bygone style of illustrative reporting, albeit redefined. Evernden does his live drawings on an A4 pad in black ink; colour comes later. He studies the socialites and editors in the audience as much as the models who parade the collections, suggesting that he enjoys portraiture and studying people as much as he does drawing clothes: 'A figure of interest is as likely to be a city gent in a Savile Row suit as a builder smoking a cigarette on a construction site.' Evernden's style is not limited to reportage, however. He is equally at home creating fictional scenery to complement the collections, and develops fantasy scenes as original compositions.

clym evernden

Prada A/W 2014–15
Created for *A Magazine Curated By*
(Belgium), 2014

Opposite
Thom Browne A/W 2014–15
Created for *A Magazine Curated By*
(Belgium), 2014

Right
Backstage
Personal work, 2014

Opposite
Photographer at Paul Smith A/W 2014–15
Personal work, January 2014

Above and right
Premier models
Created for *Vogue* (UK), 2012

ricardo fumanal

**I usually step away from a work in progress
to get proper perspective, and with that, I know
when it feels finished. Leaving something
to the imagination is important.**

Spanish illustrator Ricardo Fumanal trained in graphic and advertising design at the Municipal College of Fine Arts in Lleida, Spain, and worked as a graphic designer in Barcelona, where he also studied printing and illustration. Now living in Berlin, he has become one of the most successful and in-demand illustrators currently working in fashion, and a firm favourite with countless magazines, from *Dazed & Confused* and *Vogue Hommes Japan* to *GQ Style*, *Time*, *V Magazine* and *Hercules*.

The characteristic visual language of Fumanal's largely monochrome drawings, which are executed in pencil, pen and marker, has produced a handful of copycat illustrators, but certain of his traits are distinctively unique. He is not one simply to reproduce imagery; his skilful and intricate compositions are both playful and painstaking. The fact that his sinuous lines and precise shading are done freehand, without any pre-mapping and without using a computer, is surprising to many, given the faultless execution. The detail is so fine that, when looking at Fumanal's works up close, many viewers are fooled into thinking that they are looking at a print.

Fumanal approaches his illustrations in a highly technical way, motivated by a desire to commentate on the world of fashion as a whole. He is directly influenced by the meticulous illustrations of Aurel Schmidt, John Kleckner and Mathias Augustyniak, and the personal work of Carmen García Huerta and Charles Anastase. Fumanal also admits to hoarding fashion magazines. His work has transcended the page and screen, appearing on menswear itself, in collaborations with Lou Dalton and with Richard Nicoll for Fred Perry on the design of printed textiles.

Automatic Lover
Created for *Hercules Universal* **(USA),**
2008

Opposite
Pig's Blood and Big Boobs with Katie Eary,
Menswear Perverse New Talent
Created for *Dazed & Confused* **(UK), 2009**

This page and opposite
Automatic Lover
Created for *Hercules Universal*
(USA), 2008

Lucas Ossendrijver
Created for *Esquire Big Black Book*, 2011

Opposite
Hunting Marlon Brando
Created for *FLAUNT* (USA),
2009

Christopher Shannon
Decoy (UK), 2013

richard gray

**[I draw] people I feel really inspired by,
not just because of the way they look,
but because they're people I always perceive
as being absolutely sure of who they are,
in a really uncompromising way.**

Richard Gray's career places him as one of the most influential fashion illustrators of this century, with a client list that reads like an industry who's who. He was discovered by the late Anna Piaggi at a memorial competition for Antonio Lopez at Middlesex University (where Gray was a student) in 1988. He was soon commissioned by Piaggi for *Vanity* and *Vogue Italia*, and worked with Alexander McQueen, Vivienne Westwood and Boudicca. Gray's illustrations are in the Victoria and Albert Museum's permanent collection, and he is commissioned regularly by clients ranging from Givenchy, Antonio Berardi and Agent Provocateur to *V Magazine*, *Vogue Italia* and Ray-Ban. He has also illustrated the fashion shows of London and Paris for British national newspapers.

Gray, who lives in London, describes his ideal subject as one to whom he has 'a gut response...whom I *have* to draw, or initially just clicked with...because I found them so interesting...There's no typical "look"...just the person.' Although he has always illustrated both sexes, he has recently concentrated more and more on male figures. He describes his womenswear illustrations as narrative, whereas his drawings of menswear are 'more straightforward, more stylized portraiture and much more physical'. This reflects the undeniable erotic charge of most of his male portraits, whether the model is fully clothed in new-season Christopher Shannon, or unapologetically flaunting his masculine appeal in nothing but his underwear.

The model's frame often dominates and dictates Gray's compositions, with an emphasis on strong shoulders and an angled posture for added dynamism. The element of fantasy has always played a huge part in his work, whether it is glamorous, erotic or surreal. His illustrations never fail to capture the imagination.

richard gray

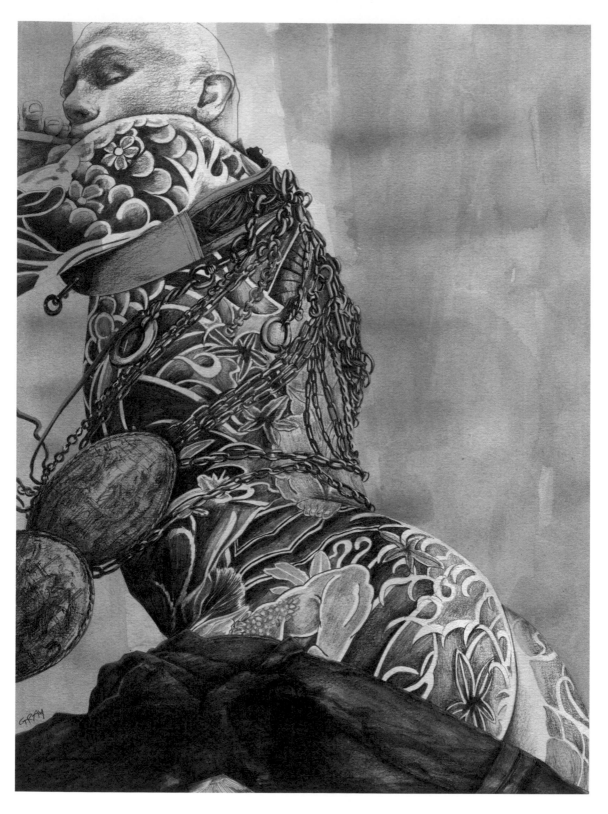

richard gray

Tattoo
Personal work, 2011

Opposite
Keko Hainswheeler jewelry
Decoy (UK), 2013

Biker (version 2)
Personal work, 2010

Opposite
Keko Hainswheeler jewelry
Decoy (UK), 2013

richard gray

Bliss
Personal work, 2010

Opposite
California
Personal work, 2010

fiongal greenlaw

**Illustrations are so important to me as this is the only
medium in which my predilection for whimsy and mythology
can truly be portrayed. It is where I can be an artist
as opposed to a designer.**

The work of Fiongal Greenlaw shows just how important creative drawing is to a fashion designer. During his menswear studies at London College of Fashion, Middlesex University and the Royal College of Art, London, his illustrations became as important as his clothing designs, and he noticed that many of the most critically supportive comments were directed at his drawings.

Greenlaw explains that he is 'attracted to those who are not typically beautiful, but would be considered unconventionally striking. I want to create the sense that these men belong to somewhere else (either historically or culturally); that they're so atypical and exotic that this is what makes them captivating to me. I've always been hugely interested in mythology.' His other influences range from such artists as Aubrey Beardsley, Alphonse Mucha and Kay Nielsen through the academic painting traditions of the late nineteenth century, including the work of Jean-Léon Gérôme and John William Waterhouse, to the cinematography of fantasy films *The Last Emperor* (1987), *The Fall* and *Pan's Labyrinth* (both 2006).

With each new clothing collection, Greenlaw attempts a new personality or zeitgeist. His illustrations are a natural way of distorting the clothes' proportions, allowing more interesting and evocative garment design. The men he draws often appear surly and melancholic. Forlorn, usually lug-eared and with foppish hair, they are surrounded by the rich decoration of mythological insignia. Subverting the idea that illustrators draw from figures or photographs, Greenlaw bases his work on imagination, believing that finding references kills the spontaneity. He sees the greatest danger of illustrating as the belief that for something to be successful it must be laboured over, and maintains that very often his best drawings are those that are quickest and most natural.

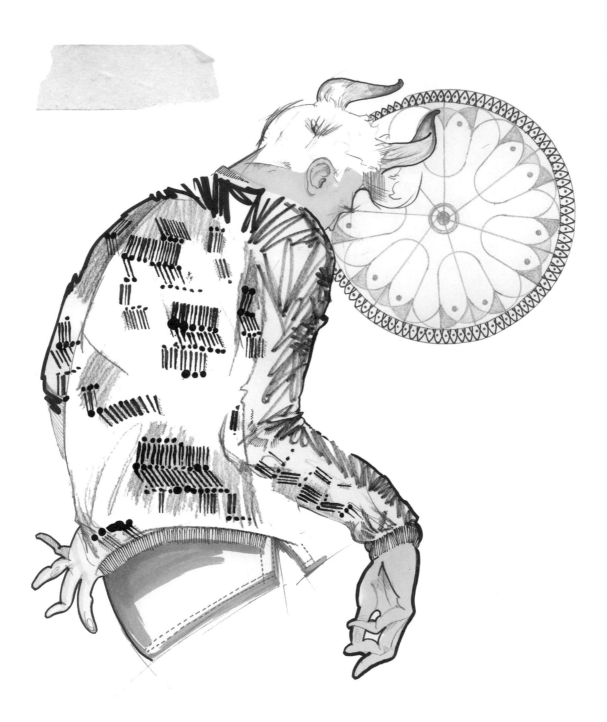

This page and opposite
DogEatDog
Personal work, 2012

Above
Fringe Frater
Personal work, 2010

Left
The 55th Road
Personal work, 2011

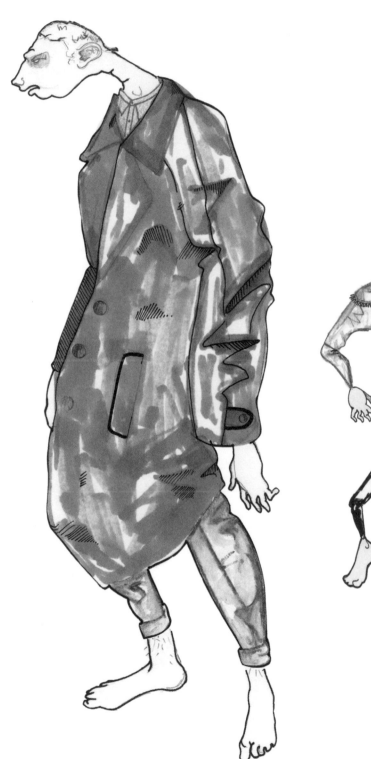
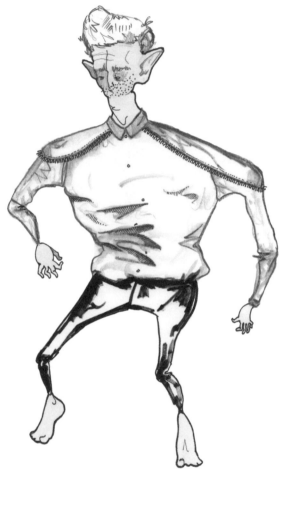

The 55th Road
Personal work, 2011

Untitled
Personal work, 2012

Opposite
Untitled
Personal work, 2014

richard haines

I'm fascinated by capturing a brief
moment – the way a guy stands, holds his coffee cup,
waits for the train. It's those very human moments
that I want to capture in line and shape.

Men are integral to the work of Richard Haines. His illustrations for his hugely successful blog, 'What I Saw Today', capture the dandies of New York, and his reportage for *GQ* magazine and the shopping site Mr Porter capture the best-dressed men both inside and outside the fashion shows of Milan, Paris and New York. Other notable clients include Prada, Calvin Klein, J.Crew, Jil Sander, the *Sunday Times Style* magazine, *GQ* and *Grazia*. Most recently, he has collaborated with Dries Van Noten on prints for the brand's Spring/Summer 2015 menswear collection.

Whether the models are posing or captured unawares, Haines's spontaneity and draughts-manship give his drawings a unique charm that has made him one of today's most prolific reportage illustrators. His skill in quickly conveying proportion and pose comes from his back-ground designing womenswear for Calvin Klein, Perry Ellis, Bill Blass and Sean Combs, where ideas are turned around at great speed and details cannot be overlooked. He collaborated with the menswear label Siki Im for its Autumn/Winter 2014 collection, in which his original illustra-tions were printed on clothing, bringing him back to his roots as designer.

In an interview with Style.com in 2013, Haines explained that he enjoys drawing both the runway outfits and members of the audience: 'There's always something to look at. If a show's not as good as it should be, there's still someone amazing sitting somewhere...I can find something riveting on a subway car.' His brisk strokes reflect the speed of live reportage: 'My work is about getting the "moment" on paper – it's about gesture and speed and immediacy.'

Haines's fascination with well-dressed but never overtly elegant men shows the sym-biotic relationship between figure and style; one cannot exist without the other. Although for studies or portraits of multiple figures he sometimes makes practice sketches, his work always appears to convey the very first captivating glimpse.

Untitled
Created for the *Sunday Times Magazine*
(UK), 2013

Opposite
Untitled
Created for Mr Porter Pitti Uomo
Style Spotter, 2013

richard haines

richard haines
124

Johan Lindeberg at *GQ* event
Personal work, 2012

Opposite
Last Sun of the Summer, Bushwick
Personal work, 2012

Luigi Tadini wears Dries Van Noten
Created for *Paper* (USA), 2012

Opposite
Christopher Hollowell in a Chair
Personal work, 2011

richard haines

128

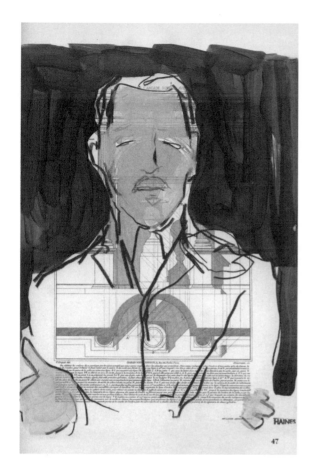

This page and opposite
Prada A/W 2012–13
Created for *Il Palazzo*, 2014

richard haines

amelie hegardt

I work mostly with female features for commercial purposes, but male features have helped me to change that train of thought. I tend to be attracted to very strong features, but it is often something else that draws your attention.

Swedish artist Amelie Hegardt is predominantly known for her stylish womenswear illustration, but her personal portraits of male models showcase her brilliant and apparently effortless use of ink, and her preoccupation with unearthing a deeper dramatic portrayal of her models. A preoccupation with beauty and the face is prevalent in her work, and it is no surprise that she has contributed to campaigns and editorials for *Vogue Hommes Japan*, Guerlain, Mac Cosmetics, Sephora and Harrods. She has lived and worked in Milan, Paris, Beijing and New York, and is currently based in London and Stockholm.

Hegardt's depiction of female models is sensual, in pastel and watercolour; since she is primarily interested in the ideas of power and seduction through beauty, there is an emphasis on their facial profiles, their trademarks of beauty and their cosmetics. By contrast, she treats her men with a stronger simplicity; her studies of the male figure are deeper and more charged. Her approach is minimalist, using sweeping, dramatic line and fading edges that give an almost ethereal impression. She currently prefers an incomplete style, one that gives the impression of being interrupted, since she favours the 'hesitation found between the unfinished lines'.

'Illustrating is important to me for two reasons,' Hegardt explains. 'One is the actual experience of it; the highlight, a state, enjoying what you do, that moment when you are drifting away into a sense of complete stillness. The other is questioning what it is that I want my drawings to say; why is this so important? I suppose that when I stop [it will be because] I've found out.'

amelie hegardt

This page and opposite
Male portraits
Personal work, 2013

Untitled
Personal work, 2013

This page and opposite
Male portraits
Personal work, 2013

amelie hegardt

liam hodges

My preferred style of illustration is a build-up of mixed media, ideally life-size...For each season or project the narrative is different, and it's nice to try and get that into the illustrations. It's more reactionary to what I'm researching.

Menswear designer Liam Hodges, with his work for Lulu Kennedy's Fashion East and MAN (initiatives that nurture emerging young designers, and whose previous discoveries include Craig Green, Christopher Kane, Jonathan Saunders and Gareth Pugh), has proved himself to be a rising star of British menswear. The truly larger-than-life illustrations for his graduate collection at the Royal College of Art, London, stood several feet high, and his presentations have been one of the most exciting elements of London Collections: Men. His signature enlarged silhouettes, built up with paint, marker pen, pastel, printed material and spray paint, nod to 1990s hip-hop culture and film, with modern details. His clothing techniques are just as artisanal and hands-on as his illustrations, featuring patchwork and fabric dye painted on with graffiti pens.

Hodges cites his influences as varying from street artists' sketchbooks and the twentieth-century American painter Robert Rauschenberg to old punk posters and 'zines. He notes that he is creating 'a luxury brand that doesn't cater for high-borns', and that is evident in his Spring/Summer 2014 collection, which was modelled at Fashion East by young men seated on a sofa drinking beer from cans – very different from the usual static method of presentation. All the models for Hodges's show were cast on the street. He also finds it helpful to photograph friends to create a certain mood, and then asks his models to use the images as references. He describes his work as focusing on 'social symbols, masculinity and confrontation'.

Hodges's drawings, which fit easily into the visual vocabulary of his design research, would be equally at home on the walls of urban cityscapes as in the pages of his portfolios. His work provides a gritty image and raw edge that are rarely seen in an industry that is largely based on exclusivity, making for a refreshingly exciting approach.

This page and opposite
Morris On, A/W 2013–14
MA pre-collection, 2013

liam hodges

liam hodges

This page and opposite
Morris On, A/W 2013–14
MA pre-collection, 2013

Mr Black, S/S 2014
Created for Holland & Sherry
look book, 2014

jack hughes

I illustrate what I want to see in the world. Cool and sophisticated, well-dressed men and women, trapped in an impossibly unattainable contemporary mid-century-inspired Utopia.

The iconography of the tailored gent provides constant inspiration for the London-based artist Jack Hughes. Since studying illustration and animation at Kingston University, London, he has worked as the in-house illustrator for ShortList Media's first daily email title for men, 'Mr Hyde', and collaborated with Topman, Burberry, Dockers and Dr. Martens. He works with the Savile Row cloth merchant Holland & Sherry on its seasonal look books, and his other clients include *Elle*, *Esquire*, Harrods, Transport for London, River Island, *Stylist* magazine, the shopping site Mr Porter, the *New York Times* and *Wired*. He has illustrated two books, which exemplify his natural gravitation towards menswear: *The Gentleman's Guide to Cocktails* (2011) and *The Gentleman's Handbook* (2013), both by the journalist Alfred Tong.

Despite his admiration for the illustrators J.C. Leyendecker and René Gruau, Hughes prefers clean lines and colours that reflect the American take on the art deco movement, which was adopted in the United States in the 1930s and 1940s as a thoroughly modern style for a modern age. The '*Mad Men*' era has had a large influence on Hughes's work, and his illustrations, while undoubtedly contemporary, sometimes feature the backdrop of New York and other imagery symbolic of mid-century.

Of his subjects, Hughes explains: 'I've always been drawn to distant-looking, effortlessly elegant figures in art and photography. There's something wonderfully nonchalant and vaguely aspirational about them, and I suppose there's a bit of that in my own work.'

Mr Blue, S/S 2014
Created for Holland & Sherry
look book, 2014

Opposite
Turquoise
Personal work, 2013

Charlie I, A/W 2014–15
Created for River Island look book, 2014

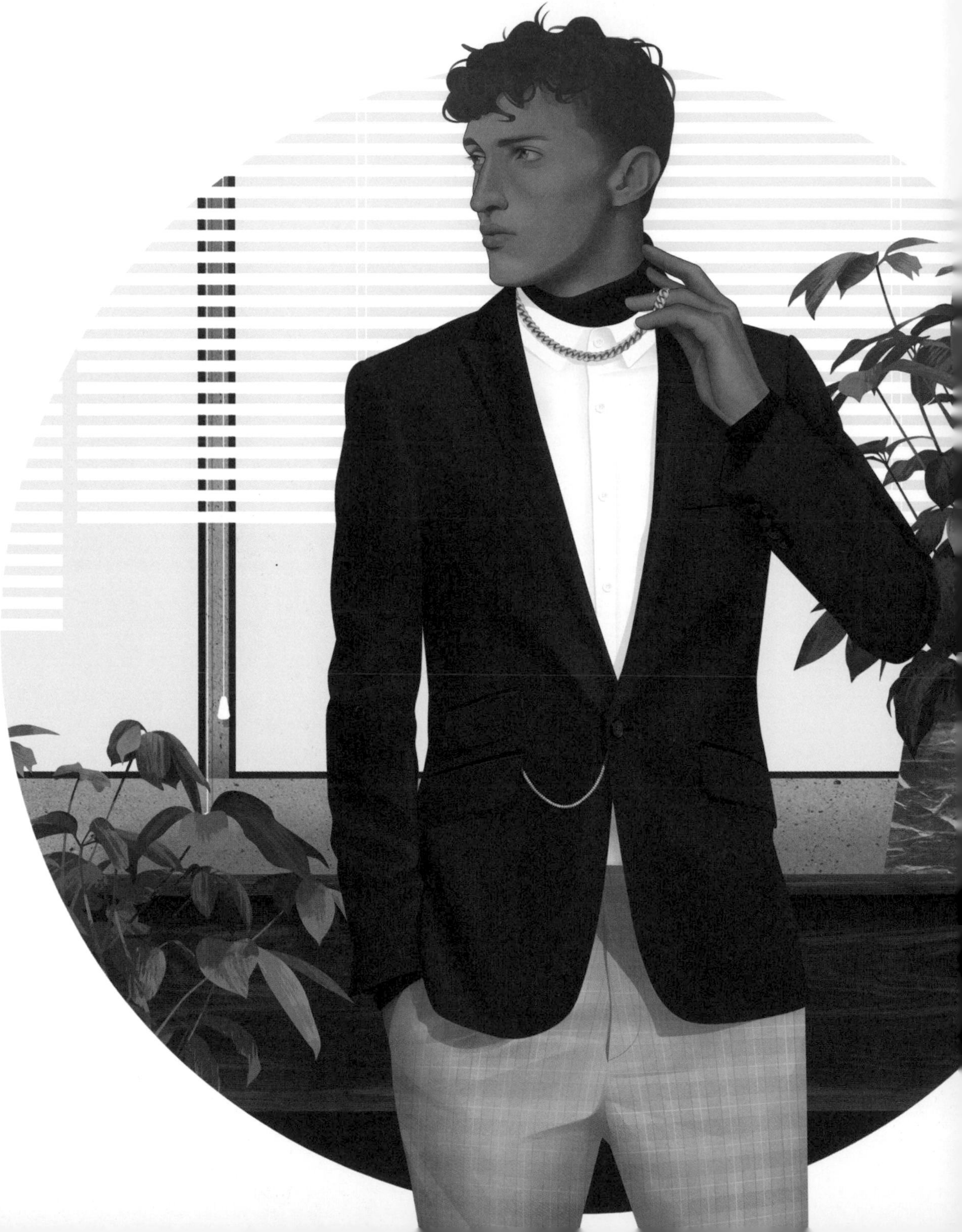

Above
Charlie II, A/W 2014–15
Created for River Island look book, 2014

Right
Sebastian, A/W 2014–15
Created for River Island look book, 2014

kareem iliya

**I'm driven by colour, texture and form, and avoid
literal interpretation. Rather than telling a story,
I focus on the fundamentals of a subject,
its minimalist form.**

Born in Beirut, Lebanon, Kareem Iliya moved to the United States at the age of nine, and is currently based in Vermont. He studied fashion design at the University of Texas, and continued his
studies at the Fashion Institute of Technology, New York. He began his fashion career working
with Giorgio Armani, and from 1992 worked freelance as an illustrator. His first commission was
the Christmas window illustrations for the Romeo Gigli boutique in New York. Iliya's client list
speaks for itself, with commissions from fashion's most prestigious brands, retailers and publications, including Louis Vuitton, Tiffany & Co., Saks Fifth Avenue, Bloomingdale's, *W Magazine*,
Harper's Bazaar, *Interview* magazine, *Vogue* and Fendi. He has worked with several prestigious
advertising agencies, and illustrated many book covers, including those for Random House's
editions of the novels of F. Scott Fitzgerald (2011).

A master of ethereal silhouette, Iliya carefully reflects the subtleties of posture and pose
in the tonal values of his watercolours and inks, and in his distinctive palette of rich, jewel-like
purples, aquas and ochres. His men are much simpler in form than their female counterparts,
who are often adorned with decorative elements such as feathered accessories, draped jewelry
and sophisticated hairstyles, revelling in a world of elegance and luxury. The men are of the
same ilk, but they are classically dressed, and at times even undressed. They represent not a
contemporary street-style man but the idealized, beautifully tailored gent. Iliya's minimalist
silhouettes remain faceless, leaving the viewer with merely an impressionistic understanding
of their lifestyles.

Untitled
Personal work, 2010

Opposite
Untitled
Personal work, 2010

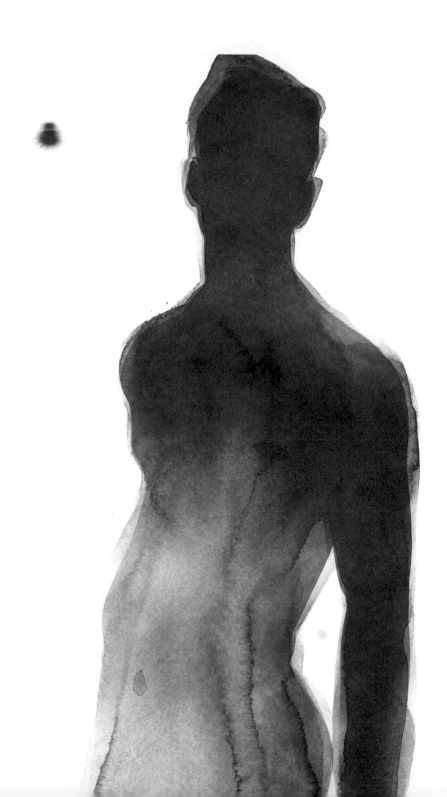

Untitled
Advertising campaign for Marriott Worldwide, 2011

Opposite
Untitled
Advertising campaign for Marriott Worldwide, 2011

Untitled
Created for Neiman Marcus, 2006

Opposite
Untitled
Personal work, 2007

jiiakuann

**When interpreting men, I tend to focus on a
mesmerizing face and succulent thighs. I'm drawn
to people who are beautiful in their own way;
it could be the face of youth, a lone silhouette smoking
under a street light or a dancing crowd in a neon glow.**

Chinese artist Kuan Jia, whose pseudonym is Jiiakuann, explains that her work is all about
visual abundance: 'A voluptuous and seductive feast for the eyes that involves vibrant colour,
a distinct alteration of physique and the serendipity of brushstroke'. Jiiakuann's illustrations
regularly grace the pages of Chinese men's magazines, including *L'Officiel Homme China* and
GQ China, and international titles including *Dorian* and *Nordic Man.* She attests that she always
enjoyed drawing girls wearing unusual clothes, and is now particularly attracted to idiosyncratic models and dramatic clothing collections.

Jiiakuann's training is in graphic design (at the University of Jiangnan, China), but illustration is her passion and watercolour her medium of choice. Rather than working in the 'watery'
tones that are associated with it, however, her scenes are vibrant, bursting with rich colour and
detail to a level not often seen in fashion illustration. The environments in which her subjects
are set are often realized to an almost overwhelming extent. Jiiakuann obtains great satisfac-
tion from the intricate drawing of ornamental pattern, and strives for painstaking detail and
a high level of realism.

An appreciation for figurative fine artists of the twentieth century is also clear in Jiiakuann's
illustrations. The fleshy studies of Lucian Freud, the red-lipped boys of Elizabeth Peyton and
the elongated torsos of Egon Schiele's figures all manifest themselves as important inspiration. In addition, her portrayal of male figures is sexually charged. While the surroundings are
filled with detail and activity and the depictions bustle with flair and colour, the characters'
expressions are by contrast serene and beguiling. This subtle juxtaposition emphasizes their
aloofness; they leave a fragile impression, yet one that comes with an arresting stare.

Prada S/S 2012
Personal work, 2013

Opposite
'Peacock' editorial
Created for *Dorian* (Sweden), 2013

jiiakuann

Boys
Personal work, 2011

Opposite
Tom Ford S/S 2013
Created for *FHM* (China), 2013

'Peacock' editorial
Created for *Dorian* (Sweden), 2013

Opposite
Louis Vuitton S/S 2013
Created for *FHM* (China), 2013

jiiakuann

Burberry Prorsum S/S 2013
Personal work, 2013

Opposite
Topman S/S 2009
Personal work, 2011

martine johanna

᷍

**What I love about drawing men is their cheekbones,
noses and dreamy faraway gazes. I prefer to draw
a contemporary version of Rhett Butler from
Gone with the Wind, who never reveals if he's into girls
or boys and is unreachable, sexy and slightly tacky.**

᷍

Despite being relatively new to drawing menswear, the Dutch artist Martine Johanna is more than familiar with interpreting handsome males, having previously carried out commissioned portraits for musicians, graphic designers and artists.

Johanna, who works as an illustrator and tutor in Amsterdam, cites high fashion, folk culture and storytelling as strong influences. After a career as a fashion designer, she changed direction in mid-2008 to focus on art and commissioned illustrations. Her style has since evolved organically to encompass detailed realism and intense colour as well as a simpler approach using negative space and line detail. Most of her works are built up from a mixture of materials: water-based oil paint, graphite or ink on wood or canvas, and sometimes simply paper and pencil.

Johanna's models often have a tripped-out demeanour, looking dazed and otherworldly. Her unique approach to drawing eyes gives the models a humble yet slightly menacing, almost alien expression. Her men are sometimes surrounded by symbolic imagery that evokes mysticism and the occult, themes that interest Johanna as a result of her upbringing and youthful imagination's journeys into fantasy: 'Even though the small village I grew up in did not accept outsider behaviour, my imagination never crumbled, exhaling my emotions in drawing, painting, dancing and creative outbursts...When I draw or paint, the world becomes translucent and fluid.'

martine johanna

Neil Krug and Leif Podhajsky
Created for *Bright Diaries* (Germany),
2014

Opposite
Shaun Samson A/W 2014–15
Created for *Unit* (Portugal), 2014

Above
Untitled (menswear S/S 2015)
Exclusive for *Menswear Illustration*, 2014

Right
Sopa
Personal work, 2009

Opposite
Thom Browne A/W 2014–15
Created for *Unit* (Portugal), 2014

martine johanna

Kuki de Salvertes of Totem Fashion
press office, 2008

jarno kettunen

I focus on capturing live, with expressive, sketch-like drawings, the essence and mood of personalities and sporadic moments, choosing my materials on the spot based on the subject and mood.

Jarno Kettunen is a Finnish illustrator, painter, draughtsman and designer who works in a captivating and spontaneous style influenced by an interest in Abstract Expressionism and Neo-Expressionism. Rather than providing information about a designer's look, his energetic works use it as a starting point for reflecting the energy, excitement and frivolity of the catwalk and the unique silhouettes of fashion models in motion. To this end he works in an unusual array of materials, including make-up, glitter and spray paint.

Kettunen studied art and graphic design at Sint-Lukas College of Visual Arts in Brussels, where he was encouraged to focus on illustration. He became more and more interested in fashion, and feels his rise to prominence came with the invitation to draw backstage at the Wendy & Jim Autumn/Winter 2007–8 show in Paris. He has honed his interest in the idea of perception by examining the work of such artists as Georg Baselitz, Willem de Kooning and Anselm Kiefer. The spontaneous work of the 1930s illustrators Christian Bérard and René Bouché is also an influence, although Kettunen's approach is raw and more direct, relying less for its modernity on descriptive line work. He believes there is a gap in fashion illustration for direct, expressive drawings that convey mood, attitude and energy rather than directly representing the clothes, and maintains that such work comes only from capturing live moments – by being backstage at fashion shows, for example.

Kettunen's work has been showcased in MoMu in Antwerp, Fashion Space Gallery in London and Gallery Nucleus in Los Angeles, and he has been commissioned by clients all over the world, including Chanel, Jean Paul Gaultier, Dior, Levi Strauss and the Royal Ballet of Flanders. His images have appeared in magazines and books including *NYLON*, *L'Officiel Maroc*, *Elle Belgium* and online at Style.com, 'Drawn' and 'A Shaded View on Fashion by Diane Pernet'.

Raw Tennis
Private commission, 2011

Opposite, top (both) and bottom left
Backstage at Kris Van Asscher A/W 2008–9
2008

Opposite, bottom right
Backstage at Dior Homme A/W 2008–9
2008

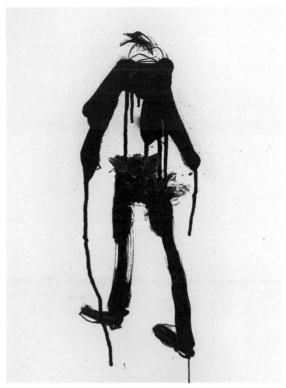

richard kilroy

**I'm always trying to draw attention to what makes
the model masculine, even if they are slim and effeminate,
such as their Adam's apple, jawline or hands.
I'm inspired by the variety of postures and
proportions men can take on.**

Richard Kilroy has been interested in drawing figures since he was a child, when he relentlessly sketched the characteristically dressed characters of the video games and cartoons he grew up with. In his teens he discovered the world of fashion illustration through the graphic appeal of Alphonse Mucha's drapery and *The Face* magazine, which was showcasing the works of Jasper Goodall, Julie Verhoeven (see page 272) and Deanne Cheuk. Other important influences were Robert Longo, for the postures in his series 'Men in the Cities'; the strong composition of Herb Ritts; and the musculature of male figures in Baroque sculpture. A graduate of Leeds College of Art, Kilroy tutors at Central Saint Martins College of Art and Design in London, and is a guest lecturer at the Royal College of Art.

Kilroy illustrates his men in photorealistic style, using graphite, which renders them in the manner of statues. Increasingly he works directly with models, selecting them for the features that have always appealed to him: a strong nose, good hands, a pronounced Adam's apple, piercing eyes and a beguiling stare. While they are men, they are still slim and young, with a boyish quality. Kilroy's style plays with negative space, suggestion and simplicity. Photorealism is combined with fluid line, and colour is used sparingly and effectively. His work is also identifiable for its detailing of garments, particularly when it comes to interpreting the surface of leather.

Among works for clients that include *Numéro* and *VMan* magazines, John Smedley and Lee Roach, Kilroy has created illustrations for Canali's shop windows across the world. In late 2010 he was one of five illustrators to be honoured with the commission for an original work for the London exhibition 'Dior Illustrated: René Gruau and the Line of Beauty'. In April 2013 a selection of his works became part of the permanent collection of fashion drawings held by the Victoria and Albert Museum in London.

richard kilroy

Thierry Mugler S/S 2013
Created for *Homme Style*, 2012

Opposite
Jil Sander S/S 2009
Personal work, 2012

Right
Lee Roach S/S 2014
Created for *A Magazine Curated By*
(Belgium), 2014

Below
J.W. Anderson cape (worn backwards)
Created for Tom Greyhound, Paris, 2014

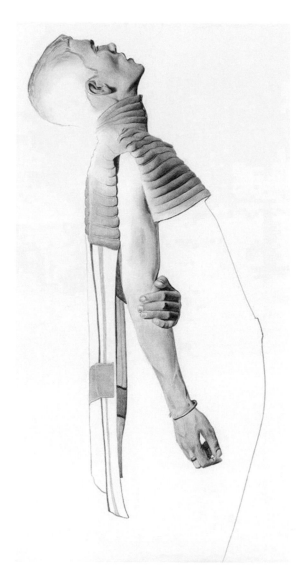

Opposite
Hugo by Hugo Boss
Created for *Decoy* (UK), 2010

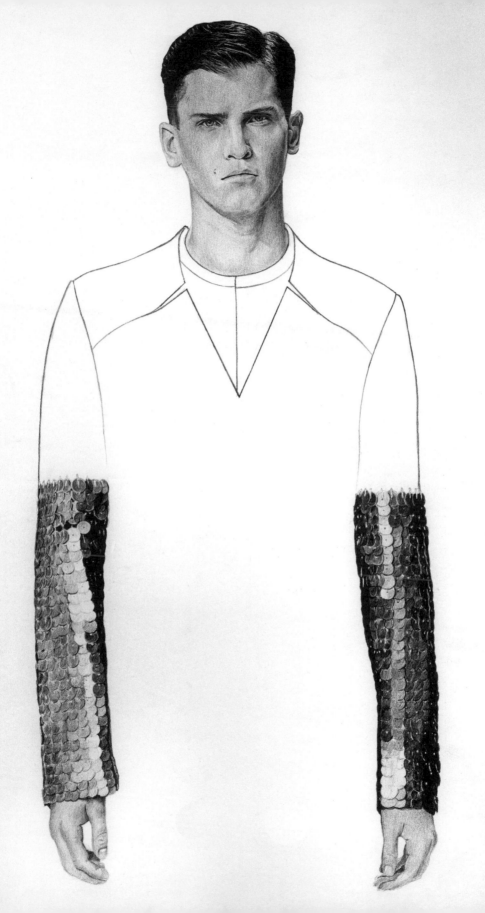

Lanvin A/W 2012–13
Personal work, 2012

Opposite
Dior Homme hat
Personal work, 2011

marco klefisch

I don't like to use professional models and usually I prefer
to use friends or strangers taken from the streets. I love big
cheekbones, huge mouths or teeth, scars or mad eyes.
Sometimes flaws are the edge of the excellence.

Milan-based artist Marco Klefisch produces advertising, live events and branded content for such cultural and commercial clients as BMW, Samsung, Microsoft and Live Nation, and his creativity ranges from drawings, graffiti and graphic design to structures and live performance. His contribution to the famously illustrated campaigns of the clothing brand Carhartt is strongly graphic, with figures and colours that are as simplistic and direct as the bold typography that features throughout. Of that collaboration, Klefisch says: 'It was very easy. They were in search of a new illustrator for their traditional visual campaign and they were in a big change of direction for the brand.' He relished the creative freedom he was given, and Carhartt's open-minded, collaborative approach.

Klefisch's work featured here, from Carhartt's Autumn/Winter 2009 and Spring/Summer 2010 campaigns, showcases what he describes as his footprint of simple compositions, crude regular strokes and sparing use of flat colour. Although he has worked as a graffiti artist, he insists that it is a separate act from his current practice. This background, however, informs an appreciation of Carhartt's streetwear ethos, as reflected in the casting for the campaign.

As the founder of a multidisciplinary space (RADIO) in Navigli, Milan, Klefisch has begun to merge his diverse experience in his recent work of live, interactive set design and visual design at large. RADIO hosts regular special events devised by guest contributors on a theme chosen by Klefisch. He also teaches creative research at the Istituto Europeo di Design (European College of Design) in Milan, running a series of workshops about the value of curiosity and research.

Edge, S/S 2010
Created for Carhartt, 2009

Hit, A/W 2009–10
Created for Carhartt, 2009

Work, A/W 2009–10
Created for Carhartt, 2009

lee song

My work comes from the weight and pressure of the individual's psychological space. Consisting of minimal space in the form and structure that can be represented today, the symbolic image of urban architecture is represented as a virtual space.

The simple yet subtly detailed work of the Korean artist Lee Song, a graduate of the College of Fine Art at Chung-Ang University in Korea, made him the choice of the fashion label Wooyoungmi for its first artistic collaboration on its international campaigns. 'Mind Games', Lee's series of works in oil on canvas, interprets pieces from the Spring/Summer 2012 collection by depicting solitary men deep in thought, their figuratively studied silhouettes isolated in the city and enhanced by surrealist landscapes that are abstract rather than literal.

Seoul-based Lee's work *Around the City* was chosen for Wooyoungmi's print campaign in 2012. Its palpable tension, with the central smashed-up car, is a break from the usual composition of menswear illustration. The troubling scene forces one to speculate about the cause of the accident, and what the statues of theorists Karl Marx and Friedrich Engels might represent. Lee's work evokes such questioning, and even sociological and psychological lamentation, on the part of the viewer.

Lee's examination of the daily routine of the modern world is greatly influenced by – although more graphically abstract than – the work of the American painter Edward Hopper, and Lee's contemporaries such as Eberhard Havekost and Carla Klein, whose realism is distinctly painterly and literal. Lee's cautious handling of colour, form and technique places his style closer to that of the Italian painter Giorgio Morandi. In common with many fashion illustrators, Lee eliminates unnecessary detail in favour of stylizing his figures and objects to create a narrative, abstract quality.

Between, 2010
From the exhibition 'Mind Games',
in collaboration with Wooyoungmi ManMade
Wooyoungmi Gallery, Seoul, 2012

Farewell, 2012
From the exhibition 'Mind Games',
in collaboration with Wooyoungmi ManMade
Wooyoungmi Gallery, Seoul, 2012

luca mantovanelli

There's always something in common between the guys I choose, the fact that they are young. There's a certain fragility in youth, and it is this sensuality that I always try to catch in my drawings.

The work of the London-based illustrator, architect and fine artist Luca Mantovanelli focuses not on clothes but rather on the male models currently in favour. He adorns his portraits with two of the most recognizable metaphors for sexuality – flowers and birds – often applied with vibrant colour. A coloured bird in flight is a loaded symbol, so it is no surprise that in a personal series Mantovanelli portrays male figures in a moment of sexual climax, the wildly coloured bird and the frames around the central figure expertly composed.

Flowers have always been a source of inspiration for figurative artists and fashion photographers; one of the latter, Robert Mapplethorpe, for example, was famed for his flower series. Flora is often applied to femininity and womenswear, and depicting a young man with flowers implies the delicacy of youth and a sensuality that is prevalent in the portrayal of adolescence. Mantovanelli's portraits of models and men in ecstasy for the likes of *Indie*, *Coitus* and *Doopler Magazine* resulted in an exclusive printed T-shirt collaboration with Givenchy in 2011. Not all Mantovanelli's subjects are portrayed as virile youth, however, as he explains: 'Melancholy is in itself fascinating through its sheer complexity, hence my relentless desire to study it further and give it a deeper consideration as an aesthetic emotion.'

Mantovanelli credits his training and practice in architecture with helping him to observe detail and proportion in his illustrations. He is best described as a portraitist, working in graphite and oils, and believes that what unites his varied influences – which range from classical Roman art and the Renaissance to Japanese manga – is their approach to line. His obsession with Luca Signorelli's *La Flagellazione* (1475) is a key example: 'The outline of the body is so strong and defined that you can really read the tension of the naked torso.' Also important are Giovanni Boldini, Edwin Austin Abbey, René Gruau, and the erotic work of Harry Bush and Paul P.

Sebastian Sauvé
Created for *Coitus* (UK), 2011

Opposite
River Viiperi
Created for *Coitus* (UK), 2011

jenny mörtsell

**I have always been drawing, since I was a kid.
The photorealistic pencil drawing style was always there,
even if I abandoned it during most of my years in college.
I started doing it again after I graduated,
and kept getting commissions.**

While photorealism may initially seem the appropriate term for the signature style of New York-based artist Jenny Mörtsell, the graphite tones and (in places) sketchier elements of her work prevent it from being too literal. It is also evident that certain outlines or details are enhanced to draw attention to and emphasize the composition of the work. The graphic cleanliness that belies her Swedish heritage (Mörtsell is from Stockholm) was honed during studies in printmaking art, graphic design and illustration, followed by a Masters in Fine Arts from Konstfack College of Arts, Crafts and Design in Stockholm in 2004.

Mörtsell adores the very different styles of the artists William-Adolphe Bouguereau, Norman Rockwell and Tom of Finland, but while their influences can be traced in her own work, she looks to photography and film for inspiration: 'Lately I've been obsessing about [Pier Paolo] Pasolini's *Teorema* [1968]. I am also a big Éric Rohmer fan.'

The magazines *NYLON*, *Elle*, *Bon*, *Cover* and *Lula*, the brands Topshop, Urban Outfitters, Whyred, Diesel and 3.1 Phillip Lim, and the *New York Times* are among Mörtsell's high-profile clients. She is equally interested in drawing men and women, but for most commissions she is not able to choose her subject. On those rare occasions that she does, a personal connection with the model matters just as much to her as their looks or style. Day to day, she carries two cameras, rather than a sketchpad, so that she can instantly capture anything that stimulates her imagination.

Knitwear
Created for Urban Outfitters, 2010

Opposite
Kangarou
Created for *L'Officiel* (France), 2010

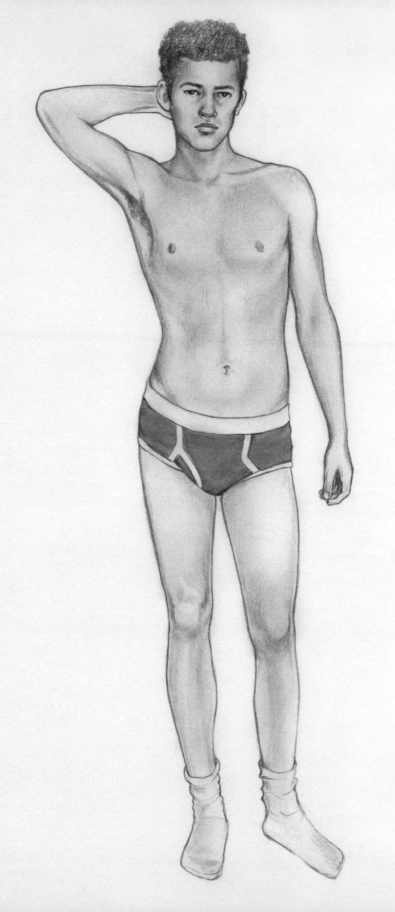

No Age (advertisement)
Created for Super Sunglasses, 2009

Benjamin
Personal work, 2011

husam el odeh

**I find men generally easier. I think this stems from
an early phase of undressed self-portraits. I suppose also,
being one myself, I have insight into the struggles of emotion,
masculinity, obligation, expectation and aggression
specific to being a man.**

Palestinian-Lebanese by descent, born and raised in Germany and a resident of the United Kingdom for some years, the versatile illustrator and jewelry designer Husam El Odeh studied Fine Art at the acclaimed Universität der Künste (University of the Arts) in Berlin. He worked as an artist in the city until 1999, when he relocated to London, drawing for *Dazed & Confused*, *QVEST* and *Vogue Hommes Japan*, and collaborating on collections with such designers as Marios Schwab and Acne Studios.

A background in craft and artisanry – he had done jewelry-making courses before deciding to take it further, and talks of his need to be constantly 'making' – is reflected in El Odeh's visual approach. Influences from the world of fine art include the twentieth-century artists Egon Schiele and Gerhard Richter. El Odeh's 'white on white' method renders his illustrations particularly subtle; a paper tone is always present despite the large daubs of paint. This sensitivity is reflected in the rounded edges of the men's profiles; these are not the hard-edged or angular faces of other artists. El Odeh believes the German side of his nature gives him a very controlled aesthetic, but admits that he likes 'inviting accidents' into his work. Realism, hinted at rather than the driving force, is combined with a deliberately painterly approach. He suggests the phrase 'romantic realism' to describe his particular combination of hard and soft, which never comes across as dramatic.

While El Odeh's ever-successful jewelry line is considered to be his main calling card (he was named Emerging Talent in Accessories at the British Fashion Awards in 2010), illustration is still part of his life. His look books feature his own drawings, and he creates personal projects: 'I chatted up a trendy bearded builder in my local coffee shop for a portrait...I also wrote and illustrated a little fairy tale last year, and again persuaded a girl in a shop to be my princess.'

husam el odeh

This page and opposite
A/W 2008–9 collections
Created for *Dazed & Confused* (UK), 2008

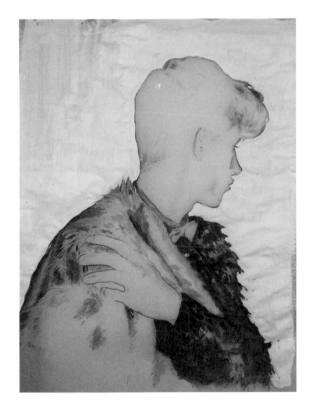

James Dean in Sweater
Created for *Vogue Hommes* (Japan), 2008

Opposite
Untitled
Created for *Boys by Girls* (UK), 2013

cédric rivrain

When I start a drawing, I work on it until I feel I have said something through it. It is at the end that I understand myself what the whole thing was about. It just needed to come out, like a story to be told.

As a child, Cédric Rivrain taught himself the basics of drawing. His father, a doctor, was an avid collector of antique medical books, anatomical illustrations, models and instruments. Rivrain describes his mother as a feminine woman who dressed in designer clothes and to whom appearance was very important. It is easy to perceive that for Rivrain, a self-taught artist who has never attended a class, drawing is his way of immortalizing the particular cultural environment provided by his parents: 'I have my inner world, and drawing is my way to make it concrete, to make it alive.'

Rivrain has produced illustrations for clients including Lanvin, Sonia Rykiel, John Galliano and Rue du Mail. Although an obsession with portraying surface texture and detail is evident in his excellent draughtsmanship, his work is better known for its distinctive mood and his focus on piercing eyes, which are often brought into the foreground with white highlights and centred within the composition, staring directly at the viewer and sometimes accentuated by masked or plaster-framed faces. Eyes are what one instinctively looks at first, and Rivrain has created a series of surreal works featuring eyes alone, disembodied and mechanized.

In his advertisements for Lanvin menswear, published exclusively in *PARIS, LA* magazine and shown here in their original full spreads, the cropping of his male figures is much more immediate than that of his female studies. The paper tones may be delicate, but the imagery is bold. The unusually coloured paper that has become one of Rivrain's calling cards sets him apart in a world where stark white backgrounds define modernity, and his illustrations are not intended to be graphic or slick; but his high-fashion subject matter, choice of model and images of disembodied, mechanized eyes fully confirm his place in the now.

Above
Raf Simons/Sterling Ruby A/W 2014–15
Personal work, 2014

Right
Harry Uzoka wears Kenzo A/W 2014–15
Personal work, 2014

Opposite
Dior Homme A/W 2014–15
Personal work, 2014

Pages 216–17
Lanvin S/S 2010 advertising campaign
Created for *Paris, LA* (France/USA), 2010

Pages 218–19
Lanvin S/S 2011 advertising campaign
Created for Paris, LA (France/USA), 2011

cédric rivrain

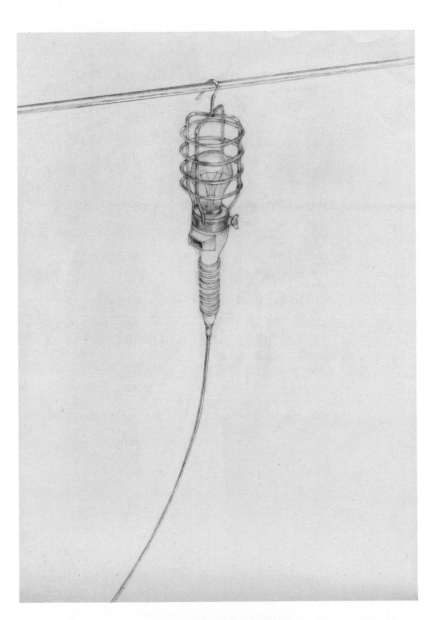

LANVIN
PARIS

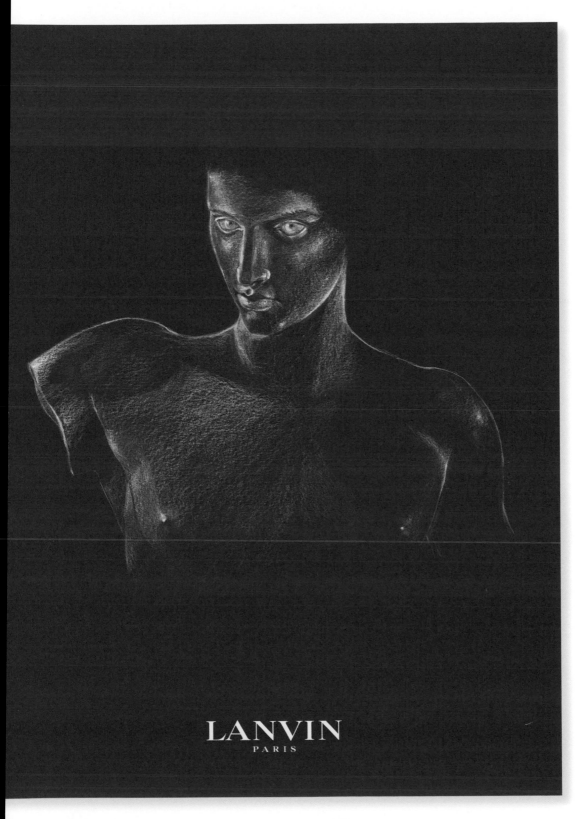

LANVIN
PARIS

cédric rivrain

felipe rojas llanos

I design with a particular type of boy in mind, drawing inspiration from characters such as Holden Caulfield from *The Catcher in the Rye*. He is a lost boy in a world he doesn't understand...a melancholic romantic.

Menswear designer Felipe Rojas Llanos was born in Chile and raised in Sweden, where he studied Fine Arts at college in Malmö before moving to London to complete his studies at Central Saint Martins College of Art and Design. He points to his BA collection there, *The Little Prince Goes to the Opera*, as the event that loosened his hand, allowing his graphic drawing style to become more fluid as a response to the interpretation of garments. He launched his eponymous clothing label after completing his MA at Central Saint Martins.

Despite his success in menswear, Rojas Llanos's superior skill as an illustrator did not go unnoticed at Central Saint Martins, to which he has been asked to return as a visiting tutor for life-drawing classes. He has the natural ease of a classic fashion illustrator, and a quickness of line coupled with an awareness of proportion. His distinctive illustrations are the result of several influences, from figurative study to a long-term fascination with graphic novels and manga animation. He also cites the cartoons *ThunderCats*, *Robotech* and *Dungeons and Dragons*, which he watched at the early age of four and five, as important to his artistic development. He has always been extremely interested in drawing and sketching, and as a child would copy the characters he saw in paperbacks or on the screen. While at secondary school he invented stories set in these worlds and inspired by folklore and mythology: 'I even drew in my checked maths books during class. I had volumes of character developments.' He now produces graphic novels for his own enjoyment, writing out the stories and creating characters. These novels, which involve people he knows in fictional scenarios, are unpublished and remain personal.

The Little Prince Goes to the Opera
Remade line-up for earlier
collection, personal work, 2014

graham samuels

**I enjoy capturing the details of clothing
but I also love how you can create a character
and tell a story about them simply by how
you choose to dress them.**

Graham Samuels approaches his fashion editorials in a uniquely narrative way that gives them the look and feel of film. His images, which are produced in a multitude of styles, have a nostalgic air that is influenced by his love of vintage commercial artworks and his collection of old LPs, books and comics. His long list of clients includes *Condé Nast Traveler*, *Elle Sweden*, the *Sunday Times*, *The Telegraph*, Soho House, *TimeOut* and *Men's Health* magazine. He was born in Essex and studied Illustration at Kingston University, subsequently completing an MA in Graphic Design and Illustration at Konstfack College of Arts, Crafts and Design in Stockholm; he now works in Sweden as an illustrator and occasional animator.

For 'Romanov Must Die', an editorial for the Swedish magazine *Fashion Tale* in 2008, Samuels was inspired by the infamous film noir directors Fritz Lang and Anthony Mann, the early films of Roman Polanski, and the twentieth-century photographers Man Ray and Jeanloup Sieff. Using white and grey pencil and paint on toned paper, he captures perfectly the subtleties of light falling on faces and clothes, against an atmospheric black backdrop. Areas of photorealism combine with unfinished, sketchier elements to show the hand of the illustrator at work. He explains: 'I approached the project as if it were a short film; I made storyboards, taking into consideration lighting, framing and telling the story economically and without words.'

Samuels's editorial 'Endurance' for *Stockholm Fashion Week Magazine* (2011) is in a very different style, influenced by the engravings of the nineteenth-century artist Gustav Doré and the dynamic, scratchy lines of Eddie Campbell's work on the graphic novel *From Hell* (1989–96). Samuels filled the page with swift pencil lines to represent tone and texture; a yellowed paper tone creates the illusion of a long-forgotten book. Far from being weighed down by the line work, the images are dynamic, capturing the story's drama and rugged arctic setting.

From the series
'Romanov Must Die'
Created for *Fashion Tale*
(Sweden), 2008

This page and opposite
From the series 'Romanov Must Die'
Created for *Fashion Tale* (Sweden), 2008

graham samuels

graham samuels

This page and opposite
From the series 'Endurance'
Created for *Stockholm Fashion Week*
(Sweden), 2011

graham samuels

michael sanderson

There's certainly a specific male archetype
I showcase in my work. I enjoy working within the
confines of masculinity; I feel it makes the designs
and aesthetic seem smarter and more refined.

The men depicted by Portland-based artist Michael Sanderson are undoubtedly masculine in both appearance and lifestyle. A world away from high fashion and the runway, it is the great outdoors of Colorado and the North American Rocky Mountains, where he grew up, that inspires him. His men appear traditional, but in the details of their clothes and environment one gets a sense of creativity: 'For guys, it's about becoming a character – that person we aspire to be, whether through power, wealth or sexuality. In menswear it's more about personal character development [than] aesthetics; and I think the men in my work demonstrate this.'

Sanderson relinquished an early ambition to be a fashion designer for the freedom of illustration, as he explained in an interview for *B Insider*: 'Being an illustrator basically allows me to design anything without any limitations at all, while making a name for myself. If I want to design a shirt, I do it. If I want to decorate a room, I can decorate any room...Anything is possible on a plain sheet of paper.'

Sanderson's clean, graphic aesthetic (created by scanning and digitally cleaning up pencil-and-ink sketches) has an unwavering confidence that befits his masculine ideal. He describes it as 'like a children's book for the adult discerning male', and cites the simple luxury of Tom Ford as an important influence. The work of the photographer Bruce Weber has been vital, a fact reflected not so much in Sanderson's casting, but in the sexual undertone of his images. His men are masculine, but not in a rugged, unassuming way. Groomed, stylized, handsome and with muscular bodies, they have great hair, stubble, muscles, body hair and tan lines, all to draw attention to their figures. The use of sexuality and nudity to market clothing is a concept that Sanderson continues to use in his work: as he puts it, 'we all get dressed to get undressed'.

This page and opposite
Untitled
Personal work, 2013

michael sanderson

Untitled
Personal work, 2013

Opposite
Mannequin with Antlers
Created for Burkman Bros, 2013

michael sanderson

shohei

**I don't have any desire to draw perfect 'Superman' characters...
We're just not as interesting without our flaws.**

Shohei studied oil painting at Tama Art University in Tokyo, but soon shifted medium to ball-point pens after he developed an affinity with this cheaper alternative in order to save money during his studies. His illustrations are easily identifiable because of this preference for the medium. The labour-intensive technique sets his work apart, its single colourway and fine detailing closer in appearance to the work of tattoo artists than conventional illustrative art.

Shohei's illustrations fuse Western and Japanese cultural references. A samurai holds a baseball bat rather than a sword; a geisha wears sunglasses more suited to a modern celebrity; and all engage in everyday activities such as skateboarding and playing electric guitar. Violence, sexuality and crass humour are constants. With an aesthetic comparable to that of Frank Miller's *Sin City*, the influence of film noir on Shohei is evident. Spaghetti westerns *The Wild Bunch* (1969) and *Bring Me the Head of Alfredo Garcia* (1974), as well as Masaki Kobayashi's *Seppuku* (1962; a black-and-white film about a *ronin* samurai and his *seppuku*, ritual suicide by self-disembowelling) are favourites.

Shohei has had several solo shows in the United States, at one of which twenty works sold in the first hour. In 2011 he told *Computer Arts*: 'I knew my work was special because of the Japanese influences...If I were to move to the States I wouldn't be inspired to draw Japanese-style illustrations. But being inspired to draw something different could be cool too.' As part of his campaign for the menswear brand Carhartt, shown here, Shohei was filmed making it, with sped-up footage of his time-consuming methods. His research materials included printed matter and photographs, and his many drafts captured models in various poses and outfits.

Carhartt S/S 2012 advertising campaign
Created for Carhartt, 2012

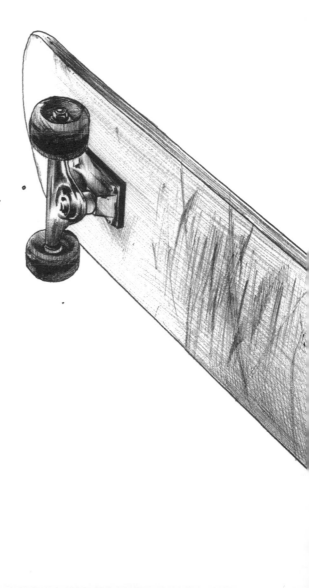

Carhartt S/S 2012 advertising campaign
Created for Carhartt, 2012

howard tangye

ˇ

**Thirty years ago, I invited someone to sit for me,
and I was aware of an energy between us; it was special,
it wasn't just superficial, and it affected the drawing.
I thought, this is the key thing...it's not just an illustration;
each one is about the individual sitter.**

The London-based artist Howard Tangye dedicated his first monograph of portraits, *Within* (2013), to his sitters. For those familiar with his work, the dedication was not surprising. A figurative artist rather than an illustrator, Tangye has always made it clear that for him his connection with his subject is the most important element of his work. His focus is to extract a certain presence from his subjects; the fashion is secondary. Yet Tangye is also very much a fashion insider: from 1997 until 2014 he was senior lecturer and head of womenswear at Central Saint Martins College of Art and Design in London. There, the Australian-born educator influenced some of the most important figures in fashion, including John Galliano, Stella McCartney, Richard Nicoll, Julie Verhoeven (see page 272) and Hussein Chalayan. Of Tangye, Galliano once said: 'He made me understand line, on the page and on the human body.'

Tangye himself began by studying fashion design at Central Saint Martins, before moving to Parsons The New School of Design in New York to focus on drawing. The combination gave him exposure to a range of people of style and presence, and established a link – which continues today – between his art and the industry.

A signature of Tangye's romanticism is his ability to describe with the expert use of colour. Rather than concentrating on realistic shading and depiction, he creates enigmatic details and textures in his portraits using a mixture of oil sticks, pastel, watercolour and ink. The expressive, outré quality he brings out in his sitters shares similarities with the work of the early twentieth-century artist Egon Schiele, but has a less aggressive, more modern take. In an interview with *A Magazine Curated by Stephen Jones* in 2013, Tangye explained: 'What I don't teach is style; I teach how the body moves and its proportions and how to make your drawings and your ideas communicate really well. But I like everybody to have his or her own style.'

howard tangye

248

Oscar
Personal work, 2014

Opposite
Matteo
Personal work, 2013

howard tangye

Phillip
Personal work, 2014

Opposite
Wes Gordon
Personal work, 2010

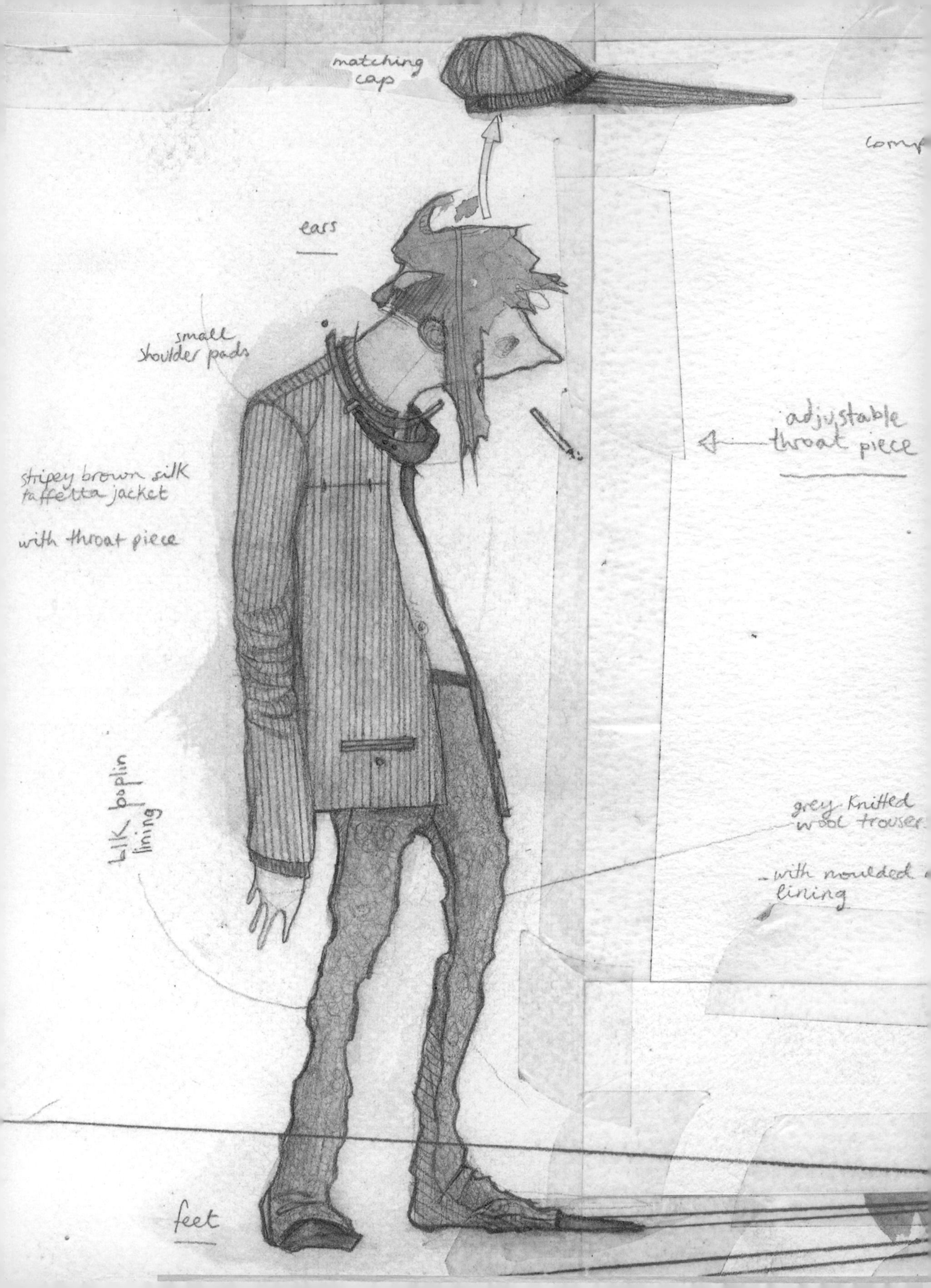

matching
cap

ears

small
shoulder pads

stripey brown silk
taffetta jacket

with throat piece

silk poplin
lining

adjustable
throat piece

grey knitted
wool trouser

with moulded
lining

feet

aitor throup

**All my work comes from drawings,
but I haven't got a clue where the fuck they come from.**

Creative director, designer, illustrator, stylist: Aitor Throup defies categorization. Having worked for publications including *Arena Homme+*, *i-D*, *VMan* and *Vogue Hommes*, and collaborated with such labels as Umbro, Stone Island and C.P. Company, it is no wonder that he has been described by the journalist Tim Blanks as one of fashion's most influential people. He was involved in the design of the England football team's kits for the World Cup in 2010, and redesigned C.P. Company's iconic Goggle jacket for its twentieth anniversary, earning a Design of the Year nomination from the Design Museum in London. Drawing is a huge part of Throup's design work, and his main interest. His blog, 'Daily Sketchbook Archives', features new sketches every day, and his images influence many menswear students, giving rise to a wave of imitators.

Throup, who was born in Buenos Aires and moved to Lancashire at the age of twelve, studied Fashion Design at Manchester Metropolitan University and Fashion Menswear at the Royal College of Art, London. At the heart of his work lies a fascination with anatomy. His drawings show not only awareness of movement, but also a reaction to it; his exaggerated characters are always in motion, twisting and contorting. His innovative design process involves creating sculptures of these bodies and draping fabric around them, part of what he calls his 'Justified Design Philosophy', by which all design features must have a reason or function.

Rather than regular collections, Throup creates conceptual projects with titles such as 'LEGS', 'Modular Anatomy' and 'Articular Anatomy'. His product line 'New Object Research' was presented at London Collections: Men in January 2013, and launched globally in shops that October. He was creative director for the musician Damon Albarn's first solo album, *Everyday Robots* (2014). In line with Throup's obsession with anatomy, the video for the single involves computer-generated scenes of cranial scans and facial reconstruction techniques.

Mongolia Preliminary Study #1
Final collection, Manchester Metropolitan
University, 2004

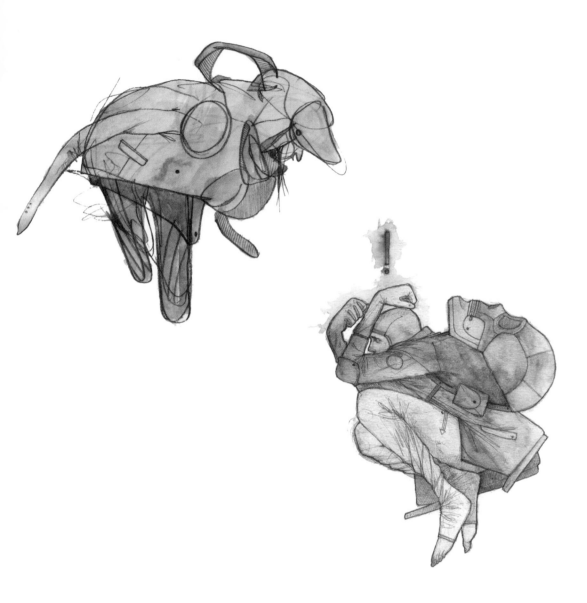

Above
Sousaphone Silhouette Analysis #1
Created for *Dazed & Confused*
(Japan), 2008

Right
On the Effects of Ethnic Stereotyping
Created for *Dazed & Confused*
(Japan), 2008

When Football Hooligans Become Hindu Gods
Final collection, Royal College of Art, London, 2006

Top
Mongolia Preliminary Overview
Final Collection, Manchester
Metropolitan University, 2004

Centre, left to right
Archive Research Project: Drill Top
(drawing and exploded view)
Created for Umbro, 2011

Bottom, left to right
Archive Research Project: Drill Trousers
(drawing and exploded view)
Created for Umbro, 2011

Still Life Overview/Mongolia Sequel Study
Entry project, Royal College of Art,
London, 2004

Zimmerli briefs
Created for *A Magazine Curated by*
Stephen Jones (Belgium), 2013

peter turner

**I always find drawing from life more
motivating and inspiring. There's an intimacy
in that ephemeral moment and it's all about
capturing that connection.**

The childhood interests of the designer and illustrator Peter Turner were a strong indicator of his future career. Not just attracted to classical art and illustration, Turner has always admired the spectacle of music, dance, photography and theatre. Learning eventually that this could be applied to fashion, he studied womenswear at Central Saint Martins College of Art and Design in London. His portfolio of drawings caught the attention of John Galliano, and on the strength of it he was offered an engagement as the in-house illustrator at Christian Dior, where he spent seven years. He attributes his illustrative style, which features couture gestures and bold strokes, to Galliano's 'limitless creativity and fearless disregard for traditional rules' and his mentoring by tutors Howard Tangye (see page 246) and Helen Beck, as well as influences ranging from Antonio Lopez and Thierry Perez to David Downton, and an appreciation of the work of 1950s commercial illustrators such as Al Parker, Tom of Finland and Harry Bush.

The influence of the greats of fashion illustration is evident in Turner's striking figurative studies and observant exaggeration of form. He says that despite his love of different media – pen, paint, crayon, oil, pastel – sometimes there is nothing better than following a line with a humble graphite pencil. As for his subjects, he finds 'flawed' people the best models: 'There's a certain vulnerability when drawing someone who is exposing their errors to you that I rarely find with professional models. As an illustrator I'm constantly looking for the unusual contour or the angled edge...I love strong, independent characters...a little eccentricity goes a long way.'

Turner now works as a designer in New York, but he still draws every day, preferring to do so for personal pleasure rather than commercially. Despite this, he is busy with private commissions and produces work to exhibit internationally. His images of men's underwear for *A Magazine Curated by Stephen Jones* (2013) are an example of his rare published work.

peter turner

Derek Rose pyjama top, Turnbull & Asser
boxer shorts (top right); Sunspel briefs (right);
Charvet boxer shorts (above)
Created for *A Magazine Curated by Stephen Jones*
(Belgium), 2013

Opposite
Falke socks
Created for *A Magazine Curated by Stephen Jones*
(Belgium), 2013

Derek Rose boxer shorts (below);
Sunspel long johns and T-shirt
(opposite)
Created for *A Magazine Curated by
Stephen Jones* (Belgium), 2013

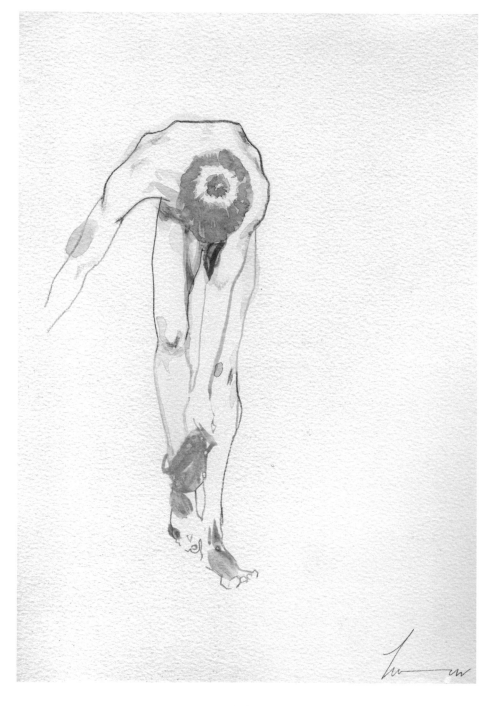

peter turner

265

Lanvin Beard, Cigarette (A/W 2009–10)
Created for *Ponystep* (UK), 2009

donald urquhart

**I will be the first to admit that they are not really
fashion illustrations, given that they do not convey fabric,
colour, texture – or even cut. In the language of my artwork
black trousers are black trousers, even when the originals
are navy, red, brown or emerald green.**

This is a typically direct and unapologetic comment from the artist Donald Urquhart, whose works certainly play with the notion of what is appropriate in fashion illustration. His images for *Ponystep* magazine provide a distinctive interpretation that allows him to continue his trademark monochromatic style. The series is pared down to black ink on white paper, anchored with typography in the form of sharp-tongued, caustic phrases or questions. Despite its apparent simplicity, his labour-intensive process involves using the smallest brushes available to maximize control of his elegant lines.

Part of London's seminal nightclub and drag scene in the 1980s (he was a contemporary of the performance artist and designer Leigh Bowery), Urquhart first showed his drawings in the series 'Peroxides on Parole' for his club night 'The Beautiful Bend', founded in the early 1990s with DJ Harvey and Sheila Tequila. A project in 2000 – for which Urquhart economized by photocopying his simplistic black-and-white images at his local Post Office – was the catalyst for a career that has included short stories, poetry, drawings, performances, radio and stage plays, and acting.

Urquhart's artwork is known for its awareness of mortality and of mainstream society's obsession with celebrity, and is permeated by a fascination with Hollywood gay icons such as Bette Davis, Judy Garland and Marilyn Monroe. His bittersweet portrayals of silver-screen starlets range from the melancholic to the darkly humorous, but Urquhart explains: 'They are heroines rather than wretched, defeated victims. There is tragedy, but there is also triumph.' His works not only act as great illustrations, but also hint at what can happen when artists engage with the portrayal of fashion.

YSL Geyser Head (A/W 2009–10)
Created for *Ponystep* (UK), 2009

Opposite
Rick Owens Nipple Sweater
(A/W 2009–10)
Created for *Ponystep* (UK), 2009

donald urquhart

Right
Comme des Garçons 'Was That It?'
(A/W 2009–10)
Created for *Ponystep* (UK), 2009

Opposite
Givenchy String Vest (A/W 2009–10)
Created for *Ponystep* (UK), 2009

Above
Dunhill Love You One Second
(A/W 2009–10)
Created for *Ponystep* (UK), 2009

julie verhoeven

I like to draw two distinct male types: either an effeminate character of ambiguous gender or an overtly brutish male, full of testosterone and grit. Deciding which to explore depends entirely on my mindset at that moment.

The monumental career of Julie Verhoeven, designer, tutor, illustrator and contemporary artist, began after a diploma in fashion at the Kent Institute of Art & Design with a job as an assistant for Martine Sitbon and John Galliano (for whom she produced in-house artwork). She created her own womenswear label, Gibo by Julie Verhoeven, in 2002. She has collaborated with Louis Vuitton and Mulberry on illustrated bags, and produced original prints for Versace womenswear, as well as editorials for such magazines as *Dazed & Confused*, *V Magazine*, *Ponystep* and *The Face*, and three monographs of her work. She has exhibited her installations, videos and mixed-media work internationally since 2002. Her success is down not just to hard work but also to her ability to diversify: the quintessential artist, she works for both herself and her clients.

The devout following Verhoeven has amassed has made her a darling of the fashion industry. A riot of vivacity and fun, she is the embodiment of her work, loved for her humility and character as much as for her dynamic and singular style. Her illustrations are revered for their wild, overt use of colour and their female characters, whose aggressive lines morph their bodies into a surreal, exaggerated vision more akin to the work of such artists as the twentieth-century German Hans Bellmer than to that of any other fashion illustrator. Since she is best known for portraying womenswear, the fact that she has produced menswear illustrations is a surprise to some people. Her trademarks still feature, but applied to a more masculine aesthetic. The squared-off shoulders and arms of some of her men are set against stern faces, while her more effeminate figures display an aloof quality. It would be easy to think that her pieces were carried out on a whim, but – while that may be true in the most literal sense – her knowledge of colour, anatomy and composition, as with any good artist, is the result of a great deal of research and inspiration, and above all of constant practice.

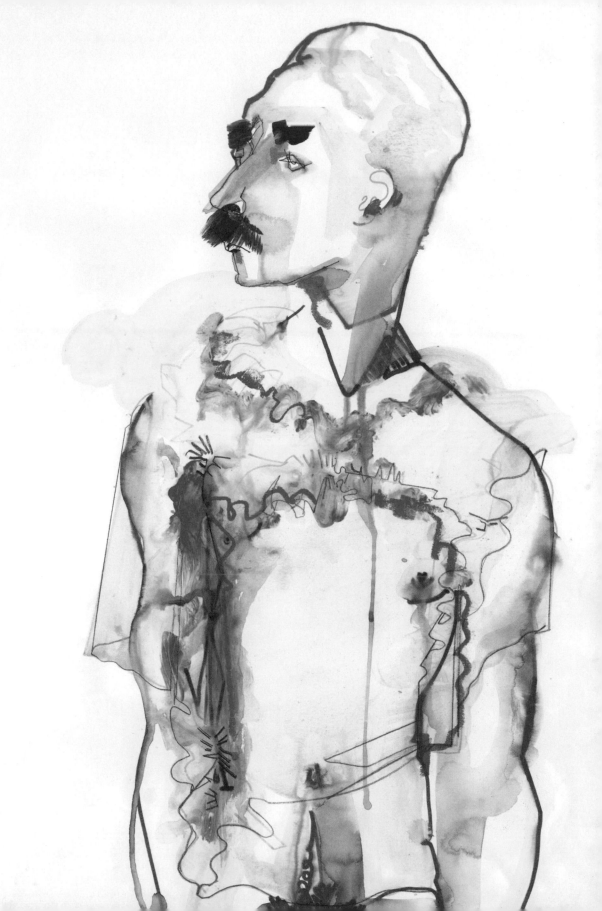

julie verhoeven

Narcissus
Personal work, 2014

Opposite
Peachy (S/S 2009)
Created for *Ponystep* (UK), 2008

Desmond
Personal work, 2014

Opposite
Jil Sander S/S 2009
Created for *Ponystep* (UK), 2008

julie verhoeven

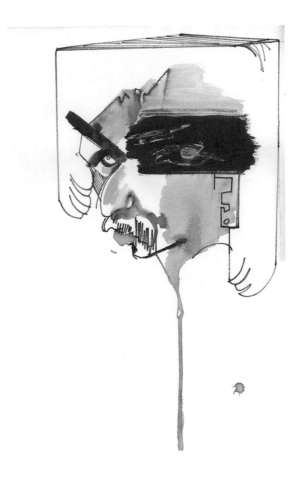

Above
Derek
Created for *Werk* (Singapore), 2012

Above, right
Comb Over
Created for *Werk* (Singapore), 2012

Opposite
Prada S/S 2009
Created for *Ponystep* (UK), 2008

john woo

I thought it would be great to visualize a dressing revolution for *Star Wars* – Darth Vader has to remove the old-fashioned calculator from his front, Jar Jar Binks has to take off his bell-bottoms – to update their wardrobe to that of stylish contemporary men.

Fictional characters from *Edward Scissorhands* (1990), *The Terminator* (1984), *Star Wars* (1977–) and *Batman* (1989) are present in each of the illustrations from John Woo's series 'He Wears It' for *I.T. Post* magazine and the online news and lifestyle magazines *Highsnobiety* and *Selectism*. Woo, a self-taught artist from Hong Kong, provides an alternative take on the 'straight-up' full-body illustrations that are commonly used for catwalk reportage and look books, depicting the outfit clearly while adding an extra dimension. Although the drawings show a humorous, light approach to the portrayal of menswear, Woo's painterly skills are not overshadowed by the famous fictional characters wearing the season's best collections. He describes how he grew up watching the *Star Wars* films: 'Those characters deeply affected me, and I was really crazy about them. I started the idea of drawing this series...My wife and I were talking about how some of our friends look like *Star Wars* characters, especially their dressing styles, such as Jar Jar Binks in his bell-bottom pants and Darth Vader always wearing black...Darth Vader is my personal favourite, so he should wear my favourite brand, Band of Outsiders. All the others [I illustrated] are also wearing the brands that I like and which match their characters.'

The notion of well-dressed superheroes, however, is not an alien one. The Metropolitan Museum of Art's exhibition 'Superheroes: Fashion and Fantasy' (2008) focused on the links between comic-book heroes and fashion, their identity through clothing and the art of power dressing. It drew attention to collections from such designers as Thierry Mugler and Azzedine Alaïa, who are inspired by the men and women in Marvel and DC comics. Woo's illustrations could be seen as merely a wardrobe update for characters whose dressing is already iconic.

Darth Vader wears Band of Outsiders
Personal work, 2010

A stormtrooper wears Thom Browne
Personal work, 2010

Boba Fett wears Supreme + Visvim
Personal work, 2010

Darth Maul wears Undercover by Jun Takahashi
Created for *Eyescream* (Japan), 2013

The Joker wears Junya Watanabe
Created for *I.T. Post* (China), 2011

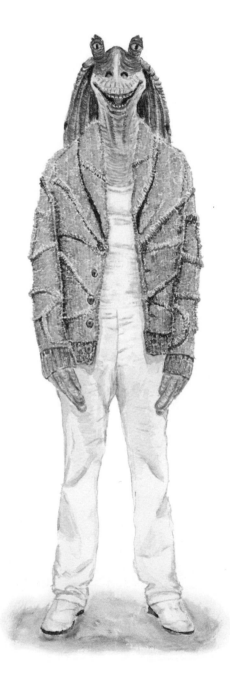

Above
A Coruscant clonetrooper wears
White Mountaineering
Created for *Highsnobiety* **(USA), 2013**

Right
Jar Jar Binks wears Maison Martin Margiela
Personal work, 2010

illustrator websites

Carlos Aponte
www.carlosaponte.com

Artaksiniya
www.artaksiniya.com

Matthew Attard Navarro
www.attardandnavarro.com

Helen Bullock
www.helenbullock.com

Gary Card
www.garycardiology.blogspot.co.uk

Guglielmo Castelli
www.guglielmocastelli.com

Sam Cotton
www.agiandsam.com

Jean-Philippe Delhomme
www.jphdelhomme.com

Stephen Doherty
www.stephenwdoherty.
carbonmade.com

Tara Dougans
www.taradougans.com

Eduard Erlikh
www.erlikh.com

Clym Evernden
www.clymdraws.com

Ricardo Fumanal
www.ricardofumanal.com

Richard Gray
www.serlinassociates.com/artist/
richardgray

Fiongal Greenlaw
www.fiongal.co.uk

Richard Haines
www.jedroot.com/illustrators/
richard-haines

Amelie Hegardt
www.ameliehegardt.com

Liam Hodges
www.liamhodges.co.uk

Jack Hughes
www.jackhughes.com

Kareem Iliya
www.kareemiliya.com

Jiiakuann
www.flickr.com/photos/
circumference

Martine Johanna
www.martinejohanna.com

Jarno Kettunen
www.jarnok.com

Richard Kilroy
www.richardkilroy.com

Marco Klefisch
www.marcoklefisch.com

Lee Song
http://blog.naver.com/ina2song

Luca Mantovanelli
www.lucamantovanelli.com

Jenny Mörtsell
www.jennysportfolio.com

Husam El Odeh
www.husamelodeh.com

Cédric Rivrain
www.cedricrivrain.com

Felipe Rojas Llanos
www.feliperojasllanos.com

Graham Samuels
www.grahamsamuels.com

Michael Sanderson
www.michaelsanderson-newyork.com

Shohei
www.hakuchi.jp

Howard Tangye
www.howardtangye.com

Aitor Throup
www.aitorthroup.com

Donald Urquhart
www.thatdonald.com

Julie Verhoeven
www.julieverhoeven.com

John Woo
www.wooszoo.com

further reading

Réjane Bargiel and Sylvie Nissen, *Gruau: Portraits of Men*, New York, 2012

Cally Blackman, *100 Years of Fashion Illustration*, London, 2007

Laird Borrelli, *Fashion Illustration by Fashion Designers*, London and San Francisco, 2008

Paul Caranicas, *Antonio's People*, London and New York, 2004

David Downton, *Masters Of Fashion Illustration*, London, 2010

Nicholas Drake, *Fashion Illustration Today*, London and New York, 1987 (rev. ed. 1994)

Mitchell Co., *Men's Fashion Illustrations from the Turn of the Century*, New York, 1990

Patrick Nagel, *Nagel: The Art Of Patrick Nagel*, New York, 1985

Roger Padilha and Mauricio Padilha, *Antonio Lopez: Fashion, Art, Sex and Disco*, New York, 2012

Juan Ramos, *Antonio: 60 70 80: Three Decades of Fashion Illustration*, London, 1995

Dean Rhys Morgan, *Bold, Beautiful and Damned: The World of 1980s Fashion Illustrator Tony Viramontes*, London, 2013

Cédric Rivrain, *Cédric Rivrain: Selected Drawings*, Paris, 2011

Angelique Spaninks, *Julie Verhoeven: A Bit of Rough*, Eindhoven, The Netherlands, 2009

Abraham Thomas, Howard Tangye, Marie McLoughlin and Louise Naunton Morgan, *Within: Howard Tangye*, Paris and London, 2013

illustration credits

All illustrations in this book are reproduced courtesy of the artist, unless otherwise credited below.

9 Victoria & Albert Museum, London
10, 11 Private collection
12 Private Collection/The Stapleton Collection/ Bridgeman Art Library
13, 14 Image courtesy The Advertising Archives

15, 16 By permission of Dean Rhys Morgan. © Estate of Tony Viramontes
18, 19 © Estate of Antonio Lopez & Juan Ramos
20 © 2014 Estate of George Stavrinos
21 © Thierry Perez
22 Courtesy of the Estate of Patrick Nagel
24, 25 Photo Daniel McMahon

acknowledgments

Firstly, I cannot say thank you enough to all the illustrators, artists and designers featured in this book, and their agents, for overcoming the hurdles of reproduction, permissions and contracts, for producing exclusive new work, and for being so helpful. It has been incredibly rewarding and exciting to collate so much inspiring work in one tome.

A massive thank you to everyone at Thames & Hudson who dealt with the project: Laura, my editor, whom I tested to the limit but who always kept me afloat – this book would be nowhere near what it is without you. Karolina, my layout artist, who has done an absolutely superb job; Maria, my picture researcher; and Rosie, my copy-editor, thank you all so much. Aoife Hanna, my assistant, helped me to focus when I had more tasks than I did fingers on my hands. Thank you to Stuart Brumfitt for taking the time to write my profile, and to Dan Thawley for writing a brilliant foreword.

To everyone else around me who suffered several months of my high stress levels, discussion, whining and enthusiasm for this project, and the people who offered me wisdom and advice or connections or just their time: my parents Moya Kilroy and Billy Kilroy, Alice Whitfield, Anthony Lee Smith, Dean Rhys Morgan, Gemma Williams, Holly Venell, Malik Al-Mahrouky, Michael O'Shaughnessy, Natalie Moran, Richard Gray, Richard Mortimer, Tara Dougans, Julie Verhoeven and anyone I could grab on the street just to start talking about it and let off steam, thank you for putting up with me! Apologies to anyone I have forgotten.